Leckie × Leckie

Scotland's leading educational publishers

T0340464

S1 to National 4
PHYSICS

PRACTICE QUESTION BOOK

Anna Lee • James Spence

00114062018

10 9 8 7 6 5 4 3 2 1

ISBN 9780008263652

Published by
Leckie & Leckie Ltd
An imprint of HarperCollins*Publishers*
Westerhill Road, Bishopbriggs, Glasgow, G64 2QT
T: 0844 576 8126   F: 0844 576 8131
leckieandleckie@harpercollins.co.uk   www.leckieandleckie.co.uk

Special thanks to
Jouve (layout and illustration); Ink Tank (cover design);
Project One Publishing Solutions (project management and editing);
Jess White (proofreading).

A CIP Catalogue record for this book is available from the British Library.

Acknowledgements
Cover photograph of British ESA Astronaut Tim Peake. Copyright: ESA/NASA.
P24 © Kitch Bain / Shutterstock.com; P26 © Lipskiy / Shutterstock.com;
P33 bestv / Shutterstock.com; P35 © TFoxFoto / Shutterstock.com;
P49 © Copacabana / Shutterstock.com; P61 © IAEA Imagebank, licensed under the Creative Commons Attribution-Share Alike 2.0 Generic license;
P74 © Jasqier, licensed under the Creative Commons Attribution-Share Alike 4.0 International license; P77 © Webspark / Shutterstock.com;
P81 © Changsgallery / Shutterstock.com

Printed and bound by CPI Group (UK) Ltd, Croydon, CR0 4YY

CONTENTS

Answers

https://collins.co.uk/pages/scottish-curriculum-free-resources

Introduction

About this book

This book provides a resource to support you in your study of physics. This book follows the structure of the Leckie and Leckie *S1 to National 4 Physics Student Book*.

Questions have been written to cover the Key areas in the Units of National 3 Physics and National 4 Physics and the Physics Experiences and Outcomes (Es and Os) of Curriculum for Excellence (CfE) Science at 3rd and 4th levels.

Features

This exercise includes coverage of

Each chapter begins with references to the **N3** or **N4** key area and the curriculum level, **CL3** or **CL4**, and the Es and Os code it covers.

Exercise 1A Renewable energy sources

> **This exercise includes coverage of:**
>
> **N3** Energy sources
> **CL3** Energy sources and sustainability SCN 3-04b
> **CL4** Energy sources and sustainability SCN 4-04a

Exercise questions

The exercises give a range of types of questions: multiple-choice; numerical; descriptive.

2 a Calculate the energy transferred when a 60 W light bulb is switched on for 3 hours.
   b Calculate the energy transferred when a 2500 W heater is switched on for 2 hours.
   c Calculate the energy transferred when a 850 W microwave is switched on for 15 minutes.

Examples

Worked example are provided for some of the numerical calculations, with supporting comments.

> **Example 9.1**
>
> A wave has a frequency of 50 000 Hz. The wavelength is $5 \cdot 0 \times 10^{-3}$ m. Calculate the speed of a wave.

frequency = 50 000 Hz

wavelength = $5 \cdot 0 \times 10^{-3}$ m = 0·005 m — (Write out what you know from the question.)

speed = frequency × wavelength — (Write out the equation (relationship).)

speed = 50 000 × 0·005 — (Substitute in what you know.)

speed = 250 m/s — (Solve for speed.)

Hint

Where appropriate, **hints** are provided to give extra support.

> **Hint** Make sure you work out the output from the NOT gate before the output from the OR gate.

Answers

Answers to all questions are provided online at:
https://collins.co.uk/pages/scottish-curriculum-free-resources

Investigation skills

This section provides help and guidance on some of the essential investigation skills you will use in your physics class.

Exercise ISA Experiments and investigations

1 These terms are all used when designing and describing investigations and experiments. State what is meant by each term.

    a aim   **b** hypothesis

    c method   **d** independent variable

    e dependent variable   **f** control variables

    g discrete data   **h** continuous data

    i conclusion   **j** evaluation

2 Why is a diagram useful when setting up an experiment?

3 Write a checklist for all the things you need to include in a method for a scientific investigation.

4 Why should you reference any information you use to help you write a scientific report?

5 Write **four** safety rules you should follow every time you are working in a laboratory?

Exercise ISB Recording and using data

1 What is the difference between accuracy and reliability?

2 Why do scientists use tables to record data?

3 A pupil collects the following results when completing an experiment. Draw a table to record their data.

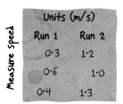

4 Calculate the averages for the values shown in this table.

Value 1	Value 2	Value 3	Value 4	Average of values
1·0	1·0	2·0	2·0	a
3·4	3·5	4·2	4·1	b
19·0	19·5	19·4	19·3	c
99·5	98·8	99·2	98·9	d
10·1	10·3	10·4	10·6	e
0·2	0·1	0·3	0·2	f
54·2	53·7	56·8	57·9	g

Exercise ISC Calculations

1 Rearrange the steps to give the correct order you should follow when working out calculations using equations.

Write the equation.

If necessary, rearrange the numbers then calculate the answer.

Write out what you know from the question.

Write the answer with the correct units.

Substitute the numbers into the equation.

2 Use the equation

voltage = current × resistance or $V = IR$

to complete this table.

voltage (V)	current (A)	resistance (Ω)
a	3·2	1·0
b	88·0	2·0
c	100·0	52·0
6·0	d	3·0
50·0	e	5·0
675·0	f	25·0
32·0	16·0	g
45·5	5.0	h
27·0	9·0	i
j	9000·0	3600·0
42·0	k	7·0
4·1	2·1	l

3 In science, we often use prefixes and scientific notation to write very large or very small numbers.

Complete this table using the correct values, prefixes or scientific notation.

Value	Using prefix	Using scientific notation
0·000 000 009 m	3 **nano**meters	
0·000 008 s	8 **micro**seconds	
	32 **milli**amperes	32×10^{-3} amperes
	4·5 **kilo**metres	$4·5 \times 10^3$ metres
1 000 000 s		$1·0 \times 10^6$ seconds
5 400 000 000 volts		$5·4 \times 10^9$ volts

4 Values should be written to the correct number of significant figures when you write the final answer to a calculation.

Complete this table, rounding each value to 2 significant figures.

Value	Rounded value to 2 significant figures
1·234 56	a
0·000 5643	b
0·0429	c
129·093	d
832 982	e
0·2389	f
432 875	g
19 874	h
0·8263	i
12·839 02	j

Exercise ISD Bar charts

1 The acronym **TAILS** can be used to help learn the important aspects of drawing bar charts and line graphs:

T	A	I	L	S
Title	Axes	Intervals	Labels	Scale

A student writes a table to shows explanations for each letter in the acronym **TAILS**. Unfortunately, the student made the table has the descriptions in the wrong places.

T	Title	Each interval increases by an equal amount, and is clearly numbered.
A	Axes	Pick the intervals so that most of the graph paper is used to plot the data.
I	Intervals	Correctly indicate what is graphed and indicate the units(in brackets).
L	Labels	Must be clear and descriptive.
S	Scale	Drawn neatly and straight.

Rewrite the table, ensuring each description is listed next to the correct term.

2 Light changes speed when it passes from one medium to another. The table shows the speed of light in various mediums.

a Show this data in a bar chart.

b State which liquid in the table slows light down the most.

c The speed of light in a vacuum is 300 000 km/s. In which medium in the table

  i is the speed of light not slowed down at all?

  ii is light slowed down the most?

Medium	Speed of light (km/s)
Air	300 000
Ice	229 000
Liquid water	226 000
Vegetable oil	204 000
Glass	197 000
Ruby	170 000
Diamond	124 000

d How much more is the light slowed down in diamond compared to ruby?

e How much more is the light slowed down in liquid water compared to ice?

3 A rubber tyre is dragged across various surfaces at a constant speed to determine the force of friction on those surfaces. The results are shown in the table.

Material tyre is dragged along	Force required (N)
Dry asphalt	63
Wet asphalt	18
Dry concrete	42
Wet concrete	32

a Construct a bar chart to display the experimental data.

b Which surface produces the greatest force of friction?

c Which surface produces the least force of friction?

d By referring to the table of data or your bar chart, suggest why concrete may be a preferred choice of surface on roads in regions with wet climates.

Exercise ISE Line graphs

1 A student conducts an experiment to determine how the number of counts of radiation varies with time for a radioactive source. The results are shown in this table.

Time (s)	Number of counts of radiation
0	80
10	55
20	40
30	28
40	20
50	15
60	10
70	7
80	5
90	4
100	3

a Draw a line graph to represent this data.

b Explain why a straight line, drawn with a ruler, would be unsuitable for this graph.

c How long did it take for the number of counts of radiation to drop to half the original value?

d Use your line graph to estimate the number of counts of radiation after 35 s.

2 A student uses an energy meter to determine how the current drawn from various electrical appliances varies with the power output of the appliance. The results are shown in the table.

Appliance	Power output (W)	Current drawn (A)
100W light bulb	100	0·43
LCD TV	60	0·26
Electric blanket	200	0·87
Coffee maker	800	3·48
Microwave	600	2·61
Vacuum cleaner	350	1·52
Iron	1100	4·78

a Explain why a line graph would be more suitable than a bar graph to find the relationship between the power output and the current drawn by each appliance.

b Construct a line graph to represent the data in the table.

c Use the graph to explain the relationship between the current drawn by an appliance and its power output.

d An electric kettle has a rated power output of 900W. Use the graph you have drawn to estimate the current drawn by the kettle.

Exercise ISF Pie charts

1 The table shows the average energy use in the home in the USA.

Type of energy use	Percentage
Entertainment	29%
Heating	9%
Washing	7%
Cooking	
Water heating	9%
Refrigeration	8%
Lighting	14%
Cooling	22%

a The percentage for cooking has been missed out. Determine how much energy is used by cooking in the USA.

b Show this data in a pie chart.

c Compare your pie chart with the one given in the example. Choose two differences, and give an explanation for why you think these differences occur.

2   The table shows the proportions of different types of radioactive waste produced by modern nuclear power stations.

Waste type	Percentage
Very low level waste	57.8%
Low level waste	34.1%
Intermediate level waste	8.0%
High level waste	0.1%

a   Work out the value of the angles required for each segment in a pie chart for this data.

b   What type of waste will be difficult to show on the pie chart? State a reason for your answer.

c   Draw a pie chart to represent this data.

3   The table shows the percentages of greenhouse gases emitted by different economic sectors in America 2014.

Sector	Percentage
Agriculture	9%
Commercial and residential	13%
Industry	22%
Transport	26%
Electricity generation	30%

a   Draw a pie chart to represent this information.

b   By referring to the pie chart, present an argument for which sector(s) should be targeted for reductions in greenhouse gas emissions.

1 Generation of electricity

Exercise 1A Renewable energy sources

This exercise includes coverage of:

N3 Energy sources
CL3 Energy sources and sustainability SCN 3-04b
CL4 Energy sources and sustainability SCN 4-04a

 1 Below are some statements about different methods of renewable energy. Match them to the correct form of renewable energy listed in the word bank.

solar power	biomass	wind power	wave power
geothermal power	hydroelectric power	tidal power	

A Water stored behind a dam is released and flows down pipes. This moving water turns a turbine and a generator, generating electricity.

B Moving air turns the blades of a turbine generating electricity.

C Crops or waste materials are burned to heat water. The water turns to steam which turns a turbine and a generator, generating electricity.

D The regular motion of the water turns a turbine and a generator, generating electricity.

E The heat energy stored in the Earth's crust heats water. The water turns to steam which turns a turbine and a generator, generating electricity.

F When light shines on photovoltaic cells, light energy is transformed into electrical energy.

G Moving water turns turbines and a generator, generating electricity.

2 State the energy changes for these different methods of generating electricity:

a hydroelectric dam   **b** wind turbine

c biomass   **d** photovoltaic (solar) panels

e wave turbines   **f** tidal power

g geothermal power.

3 Use the information in this paragraph to state **one** advantage and **one** disadvantage for wind power.

Electricity can be generated by harnessing the movement of the wind to turn turbines. Wind turbines can be installed in many locations and can vary in size from a few metres to nearly 100 metres. The output depends on the size of the turbine and the strength of the wind. If the wind is too strong it can damage the turbine.

Exercise 1B Non-renewable energy sources

1 Which of these are examples of non-renewable energy sources?

A hydroelectric dam	**B** nuclear power station
C wind turbine	**D** gas-fired power station
E biomass	**F** photovoltaic (solar) panels
G wave turbines	**H** tidal power
I geothermal power	**J** coal-fired power station

2 State **one** advantage of nuclear power stations.

3 State **one** disadvantage of nuclear power stations.

N4

4 The table shows the different ways in which electricity was generated for a country over a one-year period.

Use the information from the table to draw a pie chart to illustrate how electricity is generated in different ways.

Method of generation	Percentage (%)
Gas	36
Nuclear	4
Coal	24
Wind	18
Hydroelectric	6
Other	12

N4

5 Describe the formation of fossil fuels.

Exercise 1C Generating and distributing electricity

N4

1

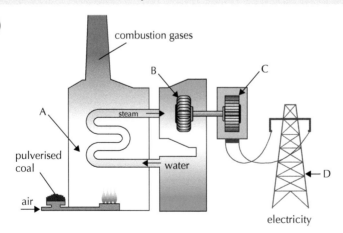

Identify the parts labelled **A, B, C** and **D** from the word bank.

turbine   **transmitting pylon**   **boiler house**   **generator**

N4 2 State the energy change that occurs when coal is burned.

N4 3 Coal is a fossil fuel used in electricity generation. Name **one** other fossil fuel used in electricity generation.

N4 4 State what happens to the water when it is heated in the boiler house of a power station.

N4 5 Explain how the different parts of the power station are used to generate electricity.

Exercise 1D Reducing the impact of energy use

This exercise includes coverage of:

N4 Generation of electricity

CL4 Topical science SCN 4-20a

N4 1 State **three** ways you can reduce the amount of fossil fuels you use.

N4 2 Give **two** reasons why it is important to conserve fossil fuels.

N4 3 A pupil wanted to investigate if solar panels (photovoltaic cells) work on cloudy days. They had access to the following apparatus:

  a photovoltaic cell   a lamp   tissue paper   connecting wires   a voltmeter

Design an experiment to find out what happens to solar panels when the weather is cloudy. Your description should include:

- a diagram to show how the apparatus was used
- what measurements were taken
- what variables should be controlled to ensure a fair test.
- any necessary safety precautions.

4 After completing the experiment described in Question 3, a pupil had this table of results.

Day	Voltage (V)			Average voltage (V)
Monday	0·14	0·23	0·11	
Tuesday	0·15	0·12	0·09	
Wednesday	0·54	0·87	0·66	
Thursday	1·23	1·52	1·30	
Friday	2·54	2·43	2·56	
Saturday	0·12	0·23	0·19	

a Calculate the average voltage for each day.

b Draw a graph of these results.

> **Hint** Days of the week are discrete variables so you should draw a bar graph. Day goes on the x-axis and average voltage goes on the y-axis.

c Which day do you think was the sunniest? Explain your answer.

d State **two** variables the pupil should keep the same to ensure this was a fair test.

2 Electrical power and efficiency

Exercise 2A Electrical power

This exercise includes coverage of:

N3 Electricity
N4 Electrical power

 1 An electric stove has this power rating label. State the power rating of the stove.

> MODEL: H40051 - 2012   2KW STOVE
>
> ---
>
> Batch No: 051203
>
> Input Voltage: 230V ~ 50Hz
> Power Consumption: 2000W
> Globatek Ltd
>
> CE RoHS Compliant

2 Power ratings are used to compare how much power different appliances use. The highest power rated devices are usually designed to convert electrical energy into heat energy, such as ovens, dishwashers and irons.

Suggest a value for the power rating of the oven.

Appliance	Power (W)
Dishwasher	1400
Hairdryer	1800
Filament lamp	100
Oven	
Power drill	750

N4 **3** State what is meant by the term **power**.

Exercise 2B Calculating power

This exercise includes coverage of:

N4 Electrical power

N4 **1** Use the relationship

$$\text{Power} = \frac{\text{energy}}{\text{time}} = \frac{E}{t}$$

to work out the missing values in this table.

Power (W)	Energy transferred (J)	Time (s)
3000	a	180
1400	b	6
150	c	3600
d	900	2·5
e	150 000	250
f	36 000 000	10 000
60	60	g
7500	675 000	h
12 500	160 000	i

> **Hint** When solving a problem using a relationship, make sure that the values used in the equation have the correct units. You may have to change time in hours or minutes to time in seconds. It may also be appropriate to leave the units as given in the question. Remember there are 3600 seconds in 1 hour.

 2

a Calculate the energy transferred when a 60 W light bulb is switched on for 3 hours.

b Calculate the energy transferred when a 2500 W heater is switched on for 2 hours.

c Calculate the energy transferred when a 850 W microwave is switched on for 15 minutes.

d Calculate the power rating of a kettle which transferred 180 000 J of energy in 60 seconds.

e Calculate the power rating of an iron which transferred 1·8 MJ of energy in half an hour.

> **Hint** The unit MJ stands for megajoules. 1 megajoule is 1 000 000 joules. To convert from MJ to J, multiply the value in MJ by 1 000 000.

f Calculate how long a 1000 W toaster was used for when it transferred 0·2 MJ of energy.

g Calculate how long it takes an immersion heater with a power rating of 50 W to transfer 10 J of energy.

Exercise 2C The cost of electricity

This exercise includes coverage of:

N3 Electricity

Example 2.1

A 0·2 kW incandescent light bulb is left on for 7 hours. The unit cost of electricity is 6 pence per kilowatt hour.

Calculate the cost (to the nearest penny) of leaving the light on for this period of time.

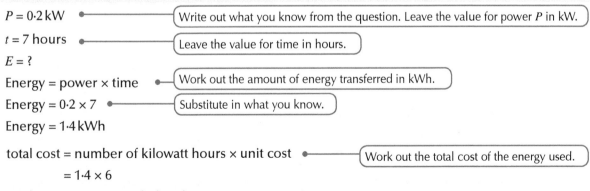

$P = 0.2$ kW ———— Write out what you know from the question. Leave the value for power P in kW.

$t = 7$ hours ———— Leave the value for time in hours.

$E = ?$

Energy = power × time ———— Work out the amount of energy transferred in kWh.

Energy = 0·2 × 7 ———— Substitute in what you know.

Energy = 1·4 kWh

total cost = number of kilowatt hours × unit cost ———— Work out the total cost of the energy used.

= 1·4 × 6

total cost = 8·4 p, rounded to the nearest penny = 8 p

1

  a A 1·6 kW kettle is used throughout the day for a total of 1·5 hours. The unit cost of electricity is 7 pence.

    Calculate the cost (to the nearest penny) of using the kettle for 1·5 hours.

  b A 0·14 kW TV is used to watch a film of 2 hours in length. The unit cost of electricity is 9 p.

    Calculate the cost (to the nearest penny) of watching the film.

  c A 1·2 kW hairdryer is used for 1 hour. The unit cost of electricity is 5·5 p.

    Calculate the cost (to the nearest penny) of using the hairdryer for 1 hour.

  d A 430 kW heater is used for 6 hours. The unit cost of electricity is 8 p.

    Calculate the cost (to the nearest penny) of using the heater for 6 hours.

Exercise 2D Efficiency

This exercise includes coverage of:

N4 Electrical power

Example 2.2

An electric motor transforms 5000 J of electrical energy into 2400 J of kinetic energy. Calculate the efficiency of the electric motor.

E_i (input energy) = 5000 J

E_o (output energy) = 2400 J   •———— (Write out what you know from the question.)

% efficiency = ?

$$\% \text{ efficiency} = \frac{\text{useful } E_o}{E_i} \times 100\%$$ •———— (Write out the equation (relationship).)

$$\% \text{ efficiency} = \frac{2400}{5000} \times 100\%$$ •———— (Substitute in what you know.)

% efficiency = 48%   •———— (Solve for % efficiency.)

 N4 **1** Use the relationship

$$\% \text{ efficiency} = \frac{\text{useful } E_o}{E_i} \times 100\%$$

to determine the missing values in the table.

Efficiency (%)	Useful energy output (J)	Total energy input (J)
a	700	1000
b	650	1950
50	**c**	2000
30	**d**	1750
75	1200	**e**
75	15	**f**

Use the relationship

$$\% \text{ efficiency} = \frac{\text{useful } P_o}{P_i} \times 100\%$$

to determine the missing values in the table.

Efficiency (%)	Useful power output (W)	Total power input (W)
a	10 000	100 000
b	40	80
50	**c**	300
10	**d**	1200
40	150 000	**e**
40	120 000 000	**f**

a A coal-fired power station uses 500 MJ of chemical energy from burning coal to produce an energy output of 125 MJ. Calculate the percentage efficiency of the power station.

b A turbine in a hydroelectric power station is 40% efficient. Calculate how much energy is transferred when 200 MJ of energy is stored in the water behind the dam.

c A system has a total input of 1·4 MJ of energy. Its output is only 1400 J. Calculate the efficiency of the system.

d A wave generator has an efficiency of 35%. Calculate the output power when the total power input is 10 MW.

e Calculate the efficiency of a system which has a total input power of 12 MW and a useful output of 3 MW.

f A kettle has an efficiency of 90%. Calculate the output power when the total power input is 1500 W.

g A microwave has an efficiency of 60%. Calculate the total power input for an output power of 720 W.

h Calculate the efficiency of a system which has a total power input of 100 MW and a useful output of 2·5 kW.

Hint	A prefix goes before the unit of measurement to help write very large or very small numbers. Don't get small m (milli) mixed up with big M (mega)!

mega	M	1 000 000	million
kilo	k	1000	thousand
milli	m	0·001	thousandth

4 Give a reason why appliances in the home are not 100% efficient.

3 Electromagnetism

Exercise 3A Magnets and magnetic fields

This exercise includes coverage of:

N3 Forces

N4 Electromagnetism

CL4 Forces SCN 4-08a

1 Copy and complete the following paragraph using the words provided.

closer   force   stronger   lines   magnetic field   region

A _ _ _ _ _ _ _ _ _ _ _ _ _ _ is the _ _ _ _ _ _ around a magnet where other magnetic materials experience a _ _ _ _ _. Magnetic field _ _ _ _ _ are used to show what the field looks like. The _ _ _ _ _ _ the field lines, the _ _ _ _ _ _ _ the magnetic field in that place.

2 These materials are placed in the magnetic field of a magnet:

iron   plastic   wood   steel   rubber   cobalt   aluminium

Create a table to show which materials are attracted to the magnet and which are not attracted to it.

3 Describe an experiment that could be used to study the field lines around a permanent bar magnet. Make sure you include:

- a list of the equipment you will need
- what observations you will make
- any safety considerations you should take.

4 Draw the magnetic field pattern around each of these magnets

a | N | S | b | | S | | N | | c | | N | | N | |

N4 **5** An experiment was carried out to determine how the strengths of various permanent magnets were affected by their temperature.

Each magnet was tested to see how many drawing pins it could pick up as the temperature was raised from 0 °C to 80 °C.

The results for three magnets are shown in the table.

	Number of drawing pins picked up by the magnet at different temperatures			
Magnet	0 °C	20 °C	50 °C	80 °C
Magnet A	27	24	18	10
Magnet B	35	31	26	19
Magnet C	31	26	18	10

a What conclusion can be drawn from the results?

b Suggest an improvement that could be made to the data collected in this experiment.

Magnet A is cooled to –20 °C.

c Predict the number of drawing pins that could be collected at this temperature.

d Which magnet has the strongest magnetic field?

e Show by calculation which magnet's strength reduced the most as it was heated.

N4 **6** Supermagnets have many useful applications, from hard disks in computers to generators in wind turbines. Describe what a supermagnet is and what they are made from.

Exercise 3B Electromagnetism

This exercise includes coverage of:

N4 Electromagnetism
CL4 Forces SCN 4-08a

N4 **1** A student passes a current through a straight piece of wire. A nearby compass needle moves.

a What exists in the region around the wire?

b The student makes the wire into a coil. The magnetic field around the wire is now stronger. What is the name given to this coil?

c Draw a sketch of this coil of wire, and include the shape of the magnetic field pattern that would exist around it.

N4 **2** A student creates an electromagnet by coiling a wire around an iron nail and connecting the wire to a battery.

a State the effect on the strength of the electromagnet when the student does the following things:

  i connects a second battery to the wire to increase the current

  ii reduces the number of turns of wire in the coil

  iii removes the iron nail from the coil.

b How does this electromagnet differ from a permanent magnet?

N4 **3** Describe **one** application of an electromagnet.

N4 **4** A pair of students complete an experiment to test the strength of an electromagnet. The graph shows their results.

a State **two** variables the students must keep constant to ensure a fair test.

b What conclusion can be drawn from the graph?

c Suggest **one** improvement the students could make to their experiment.

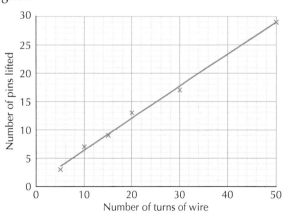

d How many drawing pins would you expect the electromagnet to pick up if the students made 40 turns of wire?

This exercise includes coverage of:

N3 Electricity

N4 Electromagnetism

CL4 Forces SCN 4-08a

  A voltmeter is connected to a coil of wire. A magnet is moved inside the coil of wire, as shown in the diagram.

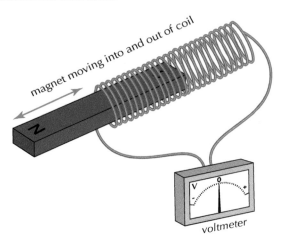

magnet moving into and out of coil

voltmeter

a Describe what happens to the needle on the voltmeter as the magnet moves.

b What does the reading on the voltmeter indicate is being produced in the coil of wire?

c When the magnet is left to sit stationary in the coil, the reading on the voltmeter is zero. What does this suggest must happen to the magnetic field to produce electricity?

2 A student uses the apparatus in Question 1 to test factors that might affect the voltage produced by moving a magnet inside a coil of wire. For each of the following changes, state what will happen to the voltage produced:

a the student uses a stronger magnet

b the student moves the magnet inside the coil faster

c the student reduces the number of coils of wire connected to the voltmeter.

3 Electric generators usually consist of a rotating coil of wire inside a magnet. The generator in a wind turbine uses the wind to turn the coil of wire. State the energy transformation in this electric generator.

N4 4 A coil of wire connected to a voltmeter is moved up and down between the poles of two magnets. A reading is observed on the voltmeter. What change could be made to increase the voltage reading?

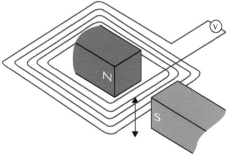

N4 5 A magnet on the end of a spring oscillates up and down inside a coil of wire. The coil of wire is connected to a voltmeter.

Describe and explain what happens to the needle on the voltmeter as the magnet moves up and down inside the coil of wire.

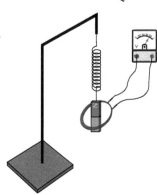

Exercise 3D Practical applications of magnets and electromagnets

This exercise includes coverage of:

N4 Electromagnetism

CL4 Forces SCN 4-08a

 1 A reed switch is a type of electrical switch that can be closed when a magnetic field is brought near to it.

It can be used with an electromagnet as shown in this circuit diagram.

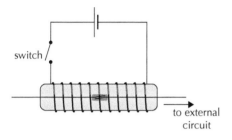

a Explain how closing the switch in the electromagnet circuit causes the reed switch to close.

b Give an example of where this type of circuit might be used.

2 The diagram shows the layout of an electric bell.

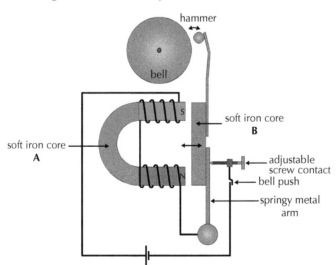

Use the word bank to complete this paragraph to explain how the bell operates.

> broken   magnetised   repeats   current   magnetism   hits   attracts

When the bell push is pressed, there is a _ _ _ _ _ _ _ in the wires. This causes the soft iron core **A** to become _ _ _ _ _ _ _ _ _ _ _, which _ _ _ _ _ _ _ _ the soft iron core **B** toward it. The hammer _ _ _ _ the bell. The contact between the soft iron core **B** and the adjustable screw contact is then _ _ _ _ _ _. This stops the current, causing soft iron core **A** to lose its _ _ _ _ _ _ _ _ _. The soft iron core **B** makes contact again with the adjustable screw and the process _ _ _ _ _ _ _.

3 Electric motors and loudspeakers use magnets or electromagnets to convert electricity into another form of energy.

    a State the energy change for:

       i an electric motor

       ii a loudspeaker.

    b For **one** of the above devices, draw a diagram of the device and explain how it operates.

Exercise 3E Using transformers in high-voltage transmission

This exercise includes coverage of:

N4 Electromagnetism

Example 3.1

In a charger for a car battery, a step-down transformer is used to decrease the voltage from 230 V to 12 V. The transformer has 5000 turns of wire in the primary coil. Calculate the number of turns in the secondary coil.

$V_P = 230\,V$ $n_P = 5000$

$V_S = 5\,V$ $n_S = ?$ ←   (Write out what you know from the question.)

$$\frac{n_S}{n_P} = \frac{V_S}{V_P}$$ ←   (Write out the equation (relationship).)

$$\frac{n_S}{5000} = \frac{5}{230}$$ ←   (Substitute in what you know.)

$$n_S = \frac{5000}{230} \times 5$$ ←   (Solve for n_S.)

$n_S = 109$ turns of wire

1

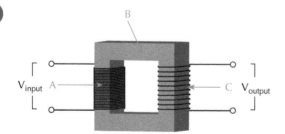

Identify the parts **A**, **B** and **C** as labelled in the diagram.

2 Write a description of how a transformer works to change the size of an a.c. voltage. Your description must include the following terms:

        alternating current   **primary coil**   **secondary coil**   **changing magnetic field**

3 State the difference between a step-up transformer and a step-down transformer.

A 5 V a.c. supply is connected to a transformer with 80 turns in the primary coil. The voltage output from the secondary coil is 600 V.

Calculate the number of turns in the secondary coil.

Use the relationship for an ideal transformer

$$\frac{n_S}{n_P} = \frac{V_S}{V_P}$$

to calculate the missing values in the table.

V_P (V)	n_P	V_S (V)	n_S
25	100	5	**a**
230	480	**b**	240
40	**c**	160	2000
d	500	12	100
25 000	280	400 000	**e**
30 000	**f**	250	40

A electric toy racing track uses a transformer to step down the voltage of the mains supply from 230 V to 5 V. The secondary coil has 1104 turns of wire.

How many turns are in the primary coil?

The lamp in a data projector uses a 12 volt supply. The projector is connected to the mains supply of 230 volts. There are 900 turns of wire in the primary coil.

How many turns are in the secondary coil?

A student is investigating the output voltage of two different transformers. Each of the two transformers has 80 turns of wire in the primary coil, but has different number of turns of wire in the secondary coil.

The student plots a graph to show how the secondary voltage varies with the primary voltage for each transformer.

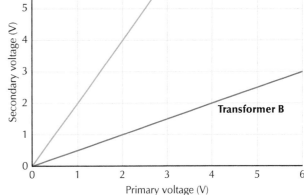

a For each transformer, state the secondary voltage when the primary voltage is 2 V.

b Use the graph to determine which transformer is a step-up transformer and which is a step-down transformer.

c Use the graph to determine the number of turns of wire in the secondary coil for:

 i transformer **A**

 ii transformer **B**.

 Remember, each transformer has 80 turns of wire in the primary coil.

4 Electrical circuits

Exercise 4A Current in a circuit

 1 A student set up this circuit to control a lamp.

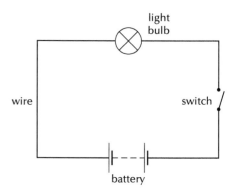

a The switch is closed and the bulb lights. The student says there is a current in the circuit. State what this means about the charges in the circuit.

b State what happens to the current in the circuit when the student opens the switch.

c Name the device the student should use to measure the current in the circuit.

d Redraw the circuit to show the correct position for this meter in the circuit.

2 a Which component in the circuit in Question 1 is used to give energy to the electric charges in the circuit?

b State the name of the electric charges that are pushed around the circuit.

c State the unit of electric current.

Exercise 4B Voltage in a circuit

 1 A student picks up an electrical cell and examines it.

a State what is meant by the word **voltage**.

b This cell is rated as 1·5 V. What does the abbreviation **V** represent?

c The student connects the cell to a light bulb using two wires. This circuit is represented by this diagram.

i State the name of the device that the student should use to measure the voltage supplied by the cell.

ii Redraw the circuit to show how such a device could be added to measure the voltage supplied by the cell.

d The student adds another cell to the circuit, next to the first cell, creating a battery.

i State the effect this has on the voltage supplied to the lamp.

ii Draw the circuit symbol for a battery.

Exercise 4C Series and parallel circuits

This exercise includes coverage of:

N4 Practical electrical and electronic circuits
CL3 Electricity SCN 3-09a

N4 **1** A student is given these electrical components:

two lamps; one cell; connecting leads

a i Draw a circuit diagram to show how the components could be connected together to create a series circuit.

ii State how many paths the current can take around the circuit.

iii One of the bulbs is unscrewed from its holder. State and explain what happens to the other bulb.

b i Draw a circuit diagram to show how the components could be connected together to create a parallel circuit.

ii State how many paths the current can take around the circuit.

iii One of the bulbs is unscrewed from its holder. State and explain what happens to the other bulb.

N4 **2** For a series circuit:

a state how the current drawn from the power supply compares with the current at different points in the circuit

b state how the voltage supplied by the power supply compares to the voltage measured across each component in the circuit.

N4 **3** A 3 V cell is connected to two lamps, L_1 and L_2, in this circuit.

An ammeter connected in series with the lamps reads 0·5 A and the voltage across lamp L_2 is 2 V.

a State the meter used to measure the voltage across lamp L_2.

b Calculate the voltage across lamp L_1.

c i What is the current in lamp L_1?

ii What is the current in lamp L_2?

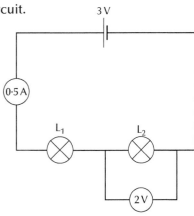

N4 **4** Determine the missing voltage (V) and current (A) values in these circuits.

a

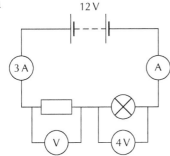

b

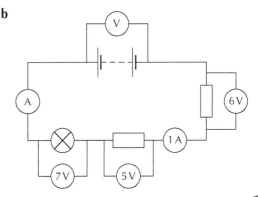

For a parallel circuit:

a state how the current leaving the power supply compares with the current through each branch of the circuit

b state how the voltage supplied by the power supply compares to the voltage across each branch of the circuit.

N4 6 This parallel circuit is set up with a 6V battery, a resistor and a light bulb.

a State the voltage across the resistor.

b State the voltage across the light bulb.

c Determine the current in the lamp.

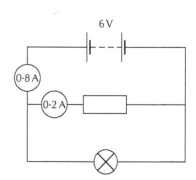

N4 7 Determine the missing voltage (V) and current (A) values in these circuits.

a

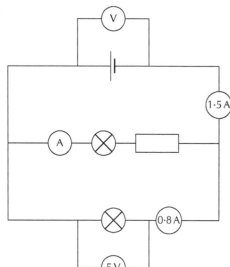

b

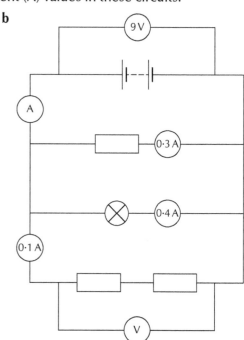

Exercise 4D Resistors in circuits

This exercise includes coverage of:

N3 Electricity

1 A pupil adds a resistor to a circuit containing a cell and a light bulb.

  a Draw the circuit symbol for a fixed resistor.

  b State what is meant by **resistance**.

  c State the units of resistance.

2 This circuit is used to control the brightness of a light bulb.

  a Identify component **X**.

  b The resistance of component **X** is increased.

    i State what happens to the brightness of the lamp.

    ii Explain how the brightness of the lamp changes. Your answer must use the words **resistance** and **current**.

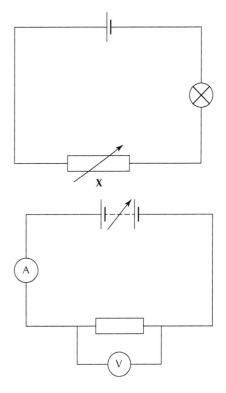

3 This circuit is set up to investigate the relationship between current, voltage and resistance.

A student varies the voltage from the power supply between 1 V and 6 V, and records the values for the current in a table.

Voltage (V)	Current (A)
1	0·2
2	0·4
3	0·6
4	
5	1·0
6	1·2

  a The student forgets to record the current in the resistor when the voltage is 4 V. Suggest what the current might be for this voltage.

  b State what happens to the current in the resistor as the voltage across the resistor is increased.

  c Suggest a reading for the current on the ammeter if the student were to increase the voltage supplied by the power supply above 6 V.

  d The student then replaces the resistor with a new resistor of a larger resistance. What do you expect will happen to the values of current that the student obtains if they repeat the experiment?

Exercise 4E Resistors and Ohm's law

> This exercise includes coverage of:
>
> **N4** Practical electrical and electronic circuits
>
> **CL4** Electricity SCN 4-09a

Example 4.1

The current in a resistor of $15\,\Omega$ is $0.4\,A$. Use Ohm's law to calculate the voltage across the resistor.

$V = ?$

$I = 0.4\,A$

$R = 15\,\Omega$ ——— (Write out what you know from the question.)

$V = IR$ ——— (Write out the equation (relationship).)

$V = 0.4 \times 15$ ——— (Substitute in what you know.)

$V = 6\,V$ ——— (Solve for V.)

N4 **1** An investigation is conducted to find out how the resistance of a wire varies with the thickness of the wire. The results are recorded in the table.

Thickness of wire (mm)	Resistance of wire (Ω)
0.46	3.1
0.38	4.5
0.32	7.0
0.27	7.8
0.23	11.0

a Use the data to plot a line graph of thickness of wire against resistance of wire.

> **Hint** Plot thickness of wire on the horizontal axis and resistance on the vertical axis.

b Use the graph to describe how the resistance of the wire is affected by the thickness of the wire.

c During this experiment, the material of each wire was kept the same. What else would the student have had to keep constant? State why this is important.

N4 **2** Three resistors are connected in series.

Use the relationship $R_T = R_1 + R_2 + R_3$ to determine the missing values in the table.

R_1 (Ω)	R_2 (Ω)	R_3 (Ω)	R_T (Ω)
10	20	30	a
150	47	2000	b
4.7	500	15	c
d	98	47	200
100	e	220	1200

N4 **3** Use the relationship $V = IR$ to find the missing values in the table.

Voltage (V)	Current (A)	Resistance (Ω)
a	2	5
b	0·5	15
12	c	200
6	0·2	d
e	0·03	500

N4 **4** A table lamp has a current of 0·40 A when connected to the mains voltage. Calculate the resistance of the wire in the table lamp.

Hint   Mains voltage is 230 V.

N4 **5** The element in a mains electric heater has a resistance of 25 Ω. Calculate the current drawn by the heater.

N4 **6** A handheld torch has a lamp with a resistance of 3 Ω and draws a current of 1·5 A. The torch uses 1·5 V cells.

Determine how many cells are needed to operate the torch.

N4 **7** An electric disk grinder is operated at mains voltage. The motor in the grinder has a resistance of 2·5 kΩ.

Calculate the current in the motor of the grinder.

N4 **8** The LED sidelights of a car each draw 200 mA. Each lamp is connected to a 12 V supply.

Calculate the resistance of one of the sidelights.

N4 **9** Calculate the reading on the meter in each of the circuits below.

a

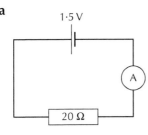

b

c

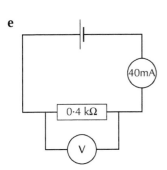

d

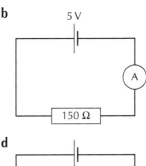

e

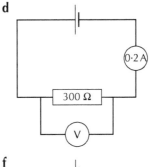

f

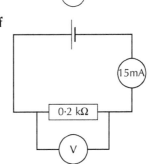

5 Batteries and cells

Exercise 5A Cells and batteries

This exercise includes coverage of:

CL3 Electricity SCN 3-10a

CL4 Electricity SCN 4-10b

1 State the difference between a cell and a battery.

2 Draw the circuit diagram for:

    a a cell   **b** a battery.

3 An early type of cell was the zinc-carbon battery.

Use the word bank to answer the questions.

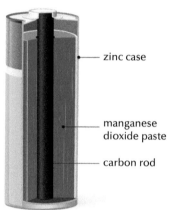

zinc case

manganese dioxide paste

carbon rod

    electrolyte   **zinc case**   **carbon rod**

    a Which part of the battery shown is the positive electrode?

    b Which part of the battery is the negative electrode?

    c What is the manganese oxide paste commonly known as?

4 Zinc-carbon batteries have largely been replaced by alkaline batteries. Search online to find out the advantages of alkaline batteries over zinc-carbon batteries.

5 Recent efforts by local councils to provide battery recycling facilities have increased. Search online to find answers to the following questions.

    a What potential problems result from disposing of used batteries in landfill sites?

    b What are the benefits of recycling used batteries?

    c What are fuel cells and how could they be used to solve the problems produced by using batteries?

Exercise 5B Fruit cells

This exercise includes coverage of:

N3 Electricity

CL3 Electricity SCN 3-10a

1 A pupil wants to investigate the voltage produced when copper and zinc metals are used with cola to create a simple chemical cell. They investigate how the area of copper and zinc immersed in the cola affects the voltage produced.

Describe an experimental method that would allow them to investigate this. Your description should include the following details:

- a list of all apparatus required
- a diagram of the experimental layout
- an explanation of how the area of the metals is controlled
- a description of how the output voltage is measured
- details of how other variables should be controlled to ensure a fair test
- any safety considerations.

2 Another pupil investigates the effect of using different fruit on the voltage produced by fruit batteries. The results are recorded in the table.

Fruit used	Voltage (V)
Banana	1·40
Apple	1·54
Orange	1·72
Kiwi	1·85

a The pupil decides a bar chart would be the most appropriate way to present the results. State a reason why this is more suitable than a line graph.

b Using graph paper, draw a bar chart of the results.

c Suggest a reason why the orange produced a higher voltage output than the banana.

Exercise 5C Photocells

This exercise includes coverage of:

N3 Electricity

1 State the energy change in a photocell.

2 Give **three** examples of applications of photocells.

3 A student conducts an investigation to determine if the surface area of a photocell affects the electrical output. They set up the photocell next to a lamp and measure its electrical output when it is covered by different sizes of black paper.

a State a device that could be used to measure the electrical output of the photocell.

b What must the student do to ensure they have conducted a fair test?

The results are recorded in the table.

Area of photocell exposed to light	Electrical output test 1	Electrical output test 2	Average electrical output
4	0·24	0·22	
8	0·51	0·49	
12	0·72	0·74	
16	0·98	1·04	
20	1·21	1·27	

c What has the student forgotten to include in the headings of the table?

d State what the student has done to increase the reliability of their results.

e Determine the average electrical output of the photocell for each area.

f Using graph paper, draw a line graph of the results.

g Describe the effect of increasing the area of the photocell exposed to light.

6 Practical electricity and safety

Exercise 6A Electrical circuits in the home

> **This exercise includes coverage of:**
>
> **N3** Electricity
>
> **N4** Practical electrical and electronic circuits
>
> **CL3** Electricity SCN 3-09a

 Modern bathrooms are wired with extractor fans as well as ceiling lamps to comply with building regulations. The circuit diagram shows the connections for the fan motor and the lamps.

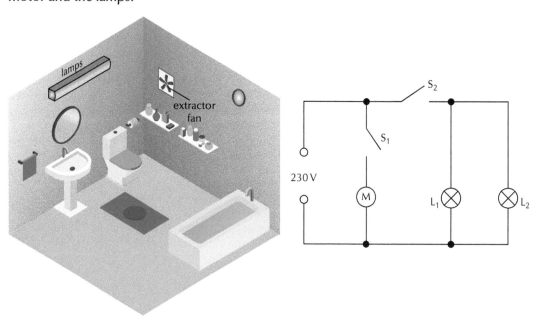

a State whether the motor or lamp L_1 or lamp L_2 will be on or off for each of these switch combinations:

  i switch S_1 closed and switch S_2 open

  ii switch S_1 open and switch S_2 open

  iii switch S_1 closed and switch S_2 closed.

b Some bathrooms are wired so that the lamps cannot be turned on unless the motor is turned on first. Redraw the circuit with switch S_1 in a new position that would enable the circuit to operate in this way.

> **Hint** Have a look at the circuit diagram for the hairdryer in Question 4.

A simplified version of the lighting circuits for a car is shown.

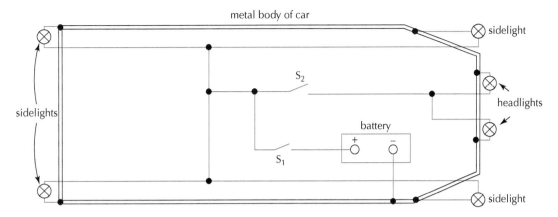

a Which switch (or switches) must be closed to turn on:

   i the sidelights

   ii the headlights.

b What is the function of the metal body of the car in the electrical circuit?

c The sidelights and headlights are wired in a parallel circuit. Explain why this is better than them being wired in series.

A circuit diagram for the wiring of a courtesy (interior) lamp in a car is shown.

a What will happen to the switch for the driver's door when the door is opened?

b Explain how the circuit enables the lamp to come on when either door is opened.

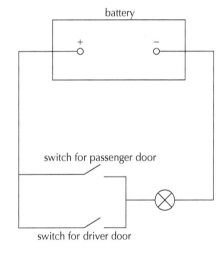

The diagram shows the electrical circuit for a hairdryer.

a Switch **A** is closed. State what happens to the hairdryer.

b The hairdryer has three heat settings: cool, warm and hot. State what setting is in operation when the following combination of switches is pressed:

   i **A** alone

   ii **A** and **B** only

   iii **A**, **B** and **C**.

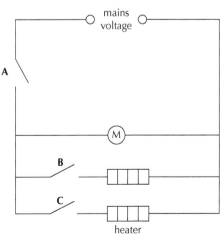

5 A variable resistor is used in the speed controller for a car racing track.

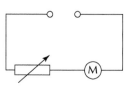

a State what type of circuit the speed controller uses.

b The speed controller is pressed to make the car go faster. Explain what happens to the resistance of the variable resistor when this happens.

c Give **one** other example of how variable resistors are used in electrical circuits in the home.

6 The diagram shows a lighting and ring mains circuit in a home.

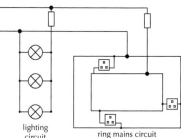

a State **one** advantage of connecting the lamps in parallel instead of series in the lighting circuit.

b The mains sockets are connected using a ring mains circuit. State **two** reasons why they are connected in this type of circuit.

c Both the lighting circuit and the ring mains circuit have fuses to protect them from high surges of current.

  i State the name given to a device that could be used to test that the fuse has not melted.

  ii Draw a circuit diagram for this device.

  iii Explain how the device can be used to test the fuse.

This exercise includes coverage of:

N3 Electricity

1 A student conducts an experiment to investigate the effect that wet hands have on the conductivity of the skin. They measure the resistance of their skin in different conditions. The results are recorded in the table.

Condition of hand	Resistance (Ω)
Dry	50 000
Wet with tap water	1000
Wet with salt water	100

a State a device the student could use to measure the resistance of the skin.

b How can the student use the measurements to draw a conclusion about the conductivity of the skin?

c Explain why salt water has a greater effect on skin resistance than tap water.

d British safety standards do not allow plug sockets to be installed in bathrooms. By referring to the results in this experiment, explain why this safety standard promotes the safe use of electrical appliances in the home.

2 The diagram shows a simplified wiring for a washing machine. The three wires of the flex are shown connected to the washing machine and wired correctly to the plug.

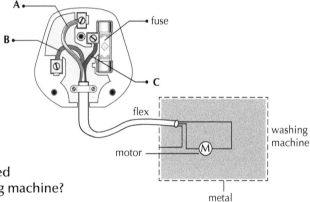

a Identify the wires labelled **A**, **B** and **C**. For each wire, state what colour the insulation is covering the wire.

b Which wire, **A**, **B** or **C**, is connected to the metal casing of the washing machine?

c The fuse is connected to wire **C**. Draw the circuit symbol for the fuse.

d A fault develops and the live wire touches the metal case of the appliance.

  i Explain why this is dangerous.

  ii Describe how the earth wire and the fuse function to make the appliance safe.

3 The diagram shows the rating plate for an electric hand mixer.

a What does the symbol of the two square boxes in the ratings plate indicate about the appliance?

b The flex connecting the hand mixer to the plug contains two wires. Name each wire in the flex.

c What type of wire is not required in this type of appliance?

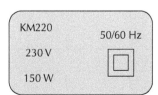

KM220
50/60 Hz
230 V
150 W

7 Electronic circuits

Exercise 7A Electrical devices

This exercise includes coverage of:

N4 Practical electrical and electronic circuits

CL4 Electricity SCN 4-09b

1 A digital thermometer is an electronic system composed of three main electronic devices.

The main devices in a digital thermometer are:

- a temperature sensor
- an LCD screen
- a microchip.

a Complete the table below to identify the sub-system each device belongs to and its purpose.

Device	Sub-system	Purpose
Temperature sensor		Measures how hot or cold the environment is
	Process	Converts the electrical signal from the temperature sensor into a temperature in °C
LCD screen		

b Draw a block diagram to show how each part of the electronic system is connected.

c Identify a device that could be used as a temperature sensor.

2 The diagrams show electrical signals that have been generated from two different output devices.

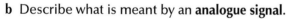

a Identify which signal is:

   i analogue   **ii** digital.

b Describe what is meant by an **analogue signal**.

c State **one** electronic output device that would produce an analogue output.

d Describe what is meant by a **digital signal**.

e State **one** electronic output device that would produce a digital output.

3 A microphone is connected to an oscilloscope to view the output of the microphone.

a Draw the circuit symbol for a microphone.

b Draw a sketch to show what the signal might look like on the oscilloscope when a person whistles into the microphone.

c Describe what happens to the signal if the person whistles louder but does not change the pitch of the note.

The word bank contains input and output devices.

> **bulb   microphone   loudspeaker   buzzer   thermistor**
>
> **motor   relay   LDR   solenoid   LED   solar cell**

Copy and complete the table to identify:

- the type of device
- whether it is analogue or digital
- the energy change for the device.

The first one has been completed for you.

Input device	Output device	Signal type	Energy transfer
–	Bulb	Analogue	Electrical to light

The graph shows how the resistance of a thermistor varies with temperature.

a State what happens to the resistance of the thermistor as the temperature increases.

b Use the graph to calculate how much the resistance of the thermistor decreases by between 28 °C and 88 °C.

c Draw the circuit symbol for a thermistor.

d State **one** electronic system that is used in the home that could make use of a thermistor as an input device.

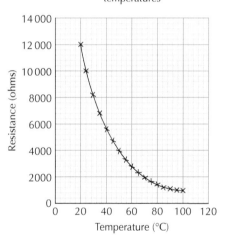

Resistance of thermistor at various temperatures

An LDR is an input device that responds to changes in light level.

a State what **LDR** stands for.

b Draw the circuit symbol for an LDR.

c What happens to the resistance of an LDR as the light level incident on it decreases?

Lamps and LEDs are both output devices that transfer electrical energy into light energy.

a What does **LED** stand for?

b Draw the circuit symbols for both the LED and the lamp.

c Which device can only be used as a digital output device? Give a reason for your answer.

d State **one** advantage the LED has over a traditional lamp.

A pupil investigates how the angle of light incident on a solar cell affects the output voltage of the solar cell. The results are recorded in the table. Note: at an angle of 0° the light was directly over the solar cell.

Angle of incidence (°)	Voltage output (V)		
	Attempt 1	Attempt 2	Average
0	4·62	4·64	
10	4·60	4·58	
20	4·57	4·59	
30	4·50	4·46	
40	4·40	4·36	
50	4·25	4·21	
60	3·70	3·60	
70	2·30	2·26	
80	0·50	0·58	

a Complete the table by calculating the average voltage output for each angle of incidence.

b Draw a line graph to show how the output voltage varies with angle of light incident on the cell.

c Describe what happens to the output voltage of the solar cell as the angle of light incident on the cell increases.

d State what this experiment tells us about how the voltage output of solar cells on the roofs of houses varies throughout the year.

e Explain why the pupil conducting the experiment repeated the data collection more than once.

N4 9 The circuit diagram shows how a relay switch is connected between a low-voltage and a high-voltage circuit.

Explain how the relay switch allows the high-voltage circuit to be operated safely.

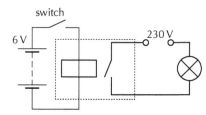

N4 10 A solenoid is an output device that converts electrical energy into kinetic energy.

a Describe the features of a solenoid.

b State **one** example of where a solenoid might be used.

Exercise 7B Switching devices

N4 Practical electrical and electronic circuits

CL4 Electricity SCN 4-09b

N4 1 A transistor is a device used to process the signal from an input device.

a Draw the circuit symbol for a transistor.

b Describe how the transistor uses the signal from an input device.

N4 **2** A transistor is connected as shown in this circuit diagram.

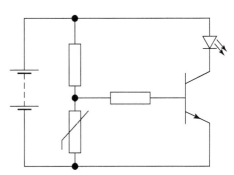

   a Identify the input device.

   b Identify the output device.

   c The transistor switches on when the temperature of the surroundings gets too low. Suggest a suitable application for this electronic system.

N4 **3** State the name of a device that can take the signal from one or two digital inputs and produce a digital output.

N4 **4** The inputs to a logic gate can be High or Low. State another name for the terms **High** and **Low**.

N4 **5** An AND gate combines the signals from two inputs to produce an output which is either High or Low.

   a Draw the symbol for an AND gate.

   b State the condition for the output of an AND gate to be logic 1.

   c Draw the truth table for an AND gate. The inputs to the AND gate can be called A and B.

N4 **6** A student draws this circuit symbol.

   a Name the logic gate that the student has drawn.

   b Draw the truth table for this logic gate.

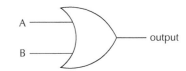

N4 **7** The NOT gate is also known as an inverter gate.

   a Draw the circuit symbol for a NOT gate.

   b Draw the truth table for the NOT gate.

   c Use the truth table to explain why the NOT gate is also known as an inverter gate.

Exercise 7C Using sensors and logic gates in electronic circuits

This exercise includes coverage of:

N4 Practical electrical and electronic circuits

CL4 Electricity SCN 4-09b

N4 **1** The diagram shows two logic gates in an electronic system.

   a Complete the truth table for this system.

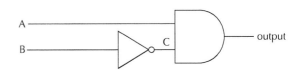

Input A	Input B	C	Output
0	0		
0	1		
1	0		
1	1		

b Input A is connected to a switch. Input B is connected to a temperature sensor.

   i State the output signal from the temperature sensor when the temperature is cold.

   ii The output of the AND gate is connected to an electric heater (via a relay). Describe **one** application of how this electronic system could be used to solve a problem.

N4 **2** **a** Draw a truth table for this combination of logic gates.

> **Hint** Make sure you work out the output from the NOT gate before the output from the OR gate.

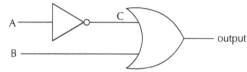

b A student wants to use the combination of gates shown in part **a** to switch on a lamp when it gets dark (light sensor input A) and when a control switch (input B) is on.

   i Will this set of logic gates allow the circuit to function as the student intends? Explain your answer.

   ii What modification can be made to enable the logic gates to operate as desired?

N4 **3** A security alarm is designed to operate if someone opens the front door to a house or steps on a pressure sensor under a mat. The diagram shows the circuit diagram for the security alarm system.

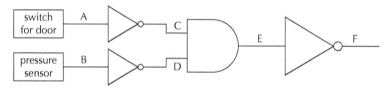

When the door is opened the logic level at A is 1.

When someone stands on the mat, the logic level at B is 1.

a Complete the truth table to show how the electronic system operates.

A	B	C	D	E	F
0	0				
0	1				
1	0				
1	1				

b The manufacturer wants to simplify the electronic system. State **one** logic gate that could be used instead of all the above gates to produce the same effect.

N4 **4** A dehumidifier is designed to extract moisture from the air, collecting the water in a container. It will turn on when the humidity of the air is above 60%. The humidity sensor gives a logic 1 when the humidity of the air is above 60%.

The container that collects the water extracted from the air has an overflow safety switch that gives a logic 1 when the container is full.

Design an electronic system using logic gates that will turn on the dehumidifier when the humidity is above 60%, and when the safety switch is off. Draw the system and explain how it operates.

8 Gas laws and the kinetic model

Exercise 8A Models of matter

 1 The three containers show particles in different states of matter.

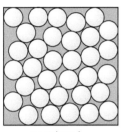 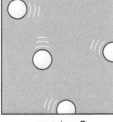 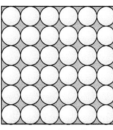

container **A** container **B** container **C**

a Which container shows the particles in:

   i a solid   **ii** a liquid   **iii** a gas?

b Describe the difference in the kinetic energy of the particles between:

   i **A** and **B**   **ii** **B** and **C**   **iii** **A** and **C**

c **i** Describe how the particles in container **A** could become more like the particles in container **B**.

   ii Describe how the particles in container **A** could become more like the particles in container **C**.

2 These materials are found in different parts of a car.

plastic gear stick	glass window	water	air
petrol	carbon dioxide	rubber tyre	engine oil

a Create a table with headings **solid**, **liquid** and **gas**, and arrange the materials correctly in the table.

b When the petrol is burned, it changes state.

   i What is the change of state?

   ii What word is used to describe this change of state?

3 The water cycle is an example of many changes of state taking place in nature. State the name given to these changes of state:

a snow changing to liquid water in the mountains

b water in the sea changing to vapour in the Earth's atmosphere

c water vapour in the atmosphere changing to form clouds.

4 When matter is heated, its temperature rises. Explain the difference between the words **heat** and **temperature**.

Example 8.1

A piece of chalk for use with a blackboard has a mass of 12·5 g and a volume of 5 cm³. Calculate its density.

$d = ?$

$m = 12·5\,g$

$v = 5\,cm^3$ ●————————————(Write out what you know from the question.)

$d = \dfrac{m}{v}$ ●————————————(Write out the equation (relationship).)

$d = \dfrac{12·5}{5}$ ●————————————(Substitute in what you know.)

$d = 2·5\,g/cm^3$ ●————————————(Solve for density.)

5 Two objects have the same volume. Object **A** has a mass of 10 g. Object **B** has a mass of 5 g. Which object will have the greatest density? Explain your answer.

6 Use the formula

$$\text{density} = \frac{\text{mass}}{\text{volume}}$$

to calculate the values of the missing quantities in this table.

Density (g/cm³)	Mass (g)	Volume (cm³)
a	200	25
b	500	400
1·0	2000	c
4·0	100	d
0·75	e	200
1·8	f	350

7 The table shows measurements of mass and volume for three different liquids.

Liquid	Mass (g)	Volume (cm³)
Mercury	204	15
Water	500	500
Paraffin oil	150	188

a Calculate the density of each of the liquids in the table.

b Each of the liquids are poured into the same large glass column. The liquids do not mix. State and explain what happens to the liquids in the column.

8 An object of dimensions $2\,cm \times 10\,cm \times 15\,cm$ is placed into water. The mass of the object is 155 g.

  a Calculate the volume of the object.

  b Calculate the density of the object.

  Water has a density of **1** g/cm³.

  c State and explain whether the object floats or sinks in the water.

Exercise 8B Heat transfer

This exercise includes coverage of:

N3 Energy transfer

CL3 Processes of the planet SCN 3-05a

1 State the main method by which heat can transfer through:

  a a solid   **b** a liquid

  c a gas   **d** a vacuum.

2 A student wrote descriptions of the three methods of heat transfer. Each description has **three** errors. Identify the errors and write suitable corrections for each one.

  a **Conduction** Conduction takes place in solids and liquids. When the particles are heated in the material, they expand causing the heat to transfer through the material. Plastic and wood are good conductors of heat.

  b **Convection** Convection takes place in gases only. When the gas is heated, the particles gain more kinetic energy and move around faster. This causes the gas to spread out, becoming more dense. This causes the gas to rise up above the cooler gas surrounding it. This movement is known as convection flow.

  c **Radiation** Radiation (or infrared radiation) takes place only in a vacuum. Objects above 100°C emit infrared radiation in straight lines and in all directions. Infrared radiation is invisible. Shiny objects emit radiation best, but black objects absorb radiation best.

3 Three students are studying an electric radiator.

  Student A thinks it transfers heat by conduction only because it is hot when they touch it.

  Student B thinks it transfers heat by convection only because it is hot above the heater.

  Student C thinks it transfers heat by radiation only because it is black.

  Use your knowledge of physics to comment on each of the students' ideas.

4 Water is brought to the boil in an electric kettle. State the main method of heat transfer:

  a i between the element of the kettle and the water

    ii throughout the water in the kettle.

  b A person touches the metal surroundings of the kettle and finds it is much hotter than the plastic handle of the kettle. Explain why this is the case.

  c When the kettle boils, the water changes to steam. Explain why the steam rises out of the spout.

5 A student is studying in their bedroom during the winter break. Feeling cold, they put on a woolly jumper and scarf.

  a Explain why the woolly jumper and scarf help the student to feel warmer.

  b The student looks around his room and writes a list of reasons why his room feels so cold:

    i solid wood floor   **ii** single-glazed window

    iii no curtains, just a blackout blind   **iv** radiator with no foil backing.

  For each item on the student's list, explain why it causes heat loss, and suggest a solution.

6 A physics class carries out an experiment to investigate heat loss in a model house. The house allows heat to transfer out through a single or double-glazed window, and also through the roof with or without loft insulation. A lamp is used as a single heat source in the centre of the model house.

  a Explain how heat loss in the home is reduced by:

    i replacing single glazing with double glazing

    ii adding loft insulation.

  b The student records the temperature rise in the loft over a period of 10 minutes with and without insulation installed. The graph shows the results of the experiment.

    i The student forgot to label each line. State which line represents the rise in temperature without insulation present in the loft. Explain your answer.

    ii The student's teacher suggests that the green data point at 6 minutes was incorrectly recorded. Explain why this may be the case.

    iii Describe two additional improvements the student could make to the graph.

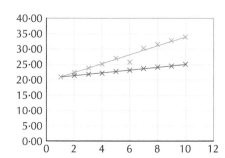

Exercise 8C Gas laws and the kinetic model

This exercise includes coverage of:

N4 Gas laws and the kinetic model

CL4 Processes of the planet SCN 4-05a

N4 **1** Use the word bank below to complete the following paragraph describing an ideal gas.

    fast   container   apart   billions

    random   collide   walls   particles

  An ideal gas is made up of _ _ _ _ _ _ _ _ of tiny _ _ _ _ _ _ _ _ _. They move about very _ _ _ _, and in _ _ _ _ _ _ directions. The particles are far _ _ _ _ _ from each other, and can _ _ _ _ _ _ _ with each other and with the _ _ _ _ _ of the _ _ _ _ _ _ _ _ _ they are in.

N4 **2** What is the name given to the theory used to explain the behaviour of gases?

The three main variables that can change for a gas are **temperature**, **volume** and **pressure**.

  a **i** What does the temperature of a gas depend on?

    ii What happens to the particles of the gas when they are heated?

  b Define what is meant by the **volume** of a gas.

  c **i** Explain how the particles of a gas create pressure.

> **Hint**   Use the words **force** and **area** in your answer to part **c**.

    ii State **two** changes in the interaction between the particles of a gas and the walls of a container that would increase the pressure of the gas.

N4 **4** The SI unit of gas pressure is pascals (Pa). State another form that this unit can take.

N4 **5** Large diggers use caterpillar tracks to prevent the digger from sinking in soft ground.

Explain why these large caterpillar tracks are used for this purpose.

N4 **6** Use the formula

$$\text{pressure} = \frac{\text{force}}{\text{area}}$$

to find the missing values in the table.

Pressure (Pa)	Force (N)	Area (m²)
a	80	2·5
b	2000	0·4
101 000	c	0·05
8600	d	0·003
15 500	1530	e
250	3500	f

N4 **7** The piston in a syringe has a cross-sectional area of 0·0004 m². A force of 15 N is applied to the piston. Calculate the pressure in the syringe.

N4 **8** The pressure of the atmosphere at sea level is 101 000 Pa. A rectangular paddling pool has a length of 3 metres and a width of 2 metres.

  a Calculate the surface area of the water in the paddling pool.

  b Calculate the force exerted by the atmosphere on the surface of the water in the paddling pool.

N4 9
The gas pressure inside an aerosol can is five times that of atmospheric pressure at sea level.

a Determine the gas pressure inside the aerosol can.

b The area of the base of the aerosol can is 0·002 m². Calculate the force that the particles in the gas exert on the base of the can.

> **Hint** The value for atmospheric pressure at sea level is given in Question 8.

N4 10
PSI is an alternative unit of air pressure often used for vehicle tyres. One PSI is equivalent to 6895 Pa. A bicycle tyre is pumped to an air pressure of 60 PSI above the pressure of the atmosphere.

a Calculate the air pressure in the tyre in pascals.

> **Hint** Remember to add the value of atmospheric pressure at sea level after converting PSI to pascals.

b Determine the force on a square section of the tyre with dimensions 1 cm × 1 cm.

> **Hint** Convert 1 cm into 0·01 m and work out the area in m².

N4 11
The apparatus in the diagram is used to investigate how the pressure in a gas varies with volume.

a State what happens to the readings on the pressure gauge as the volume decreases.

b Using the kinetic model of gases, explain the pressure change as the volume decreases.

c State **two** variables that should remain constant in this experiment.

12 The diagram shows apparatus used to investigate the relationship between temperature and pressure for an ideal gas.

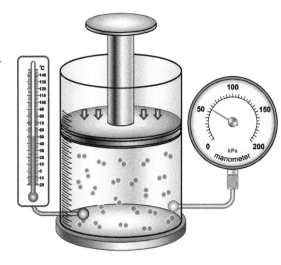

A Bunsen burner is used to heat the gas.

a State what happens to the speed of the gas particles as they are heated.

b State what happens to the kinetic energy of the gas particles as they are heated.

c Describe the effect that the change in kinetic energy of the particles has on the collisions with the walls of the container.

d What happens to the reading on the pressure gauge as the temperature of the gas increases?

e State what the person conducting the experiment must ensure happens to the piston that is pushing down on the gas as it is heated.

13 The diagram shows the apparatus used to explore the relationship between temperature and volume of a gas.

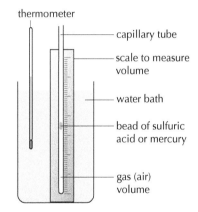

The water bath is heated using a Bunsen flame. As the temperature of the water increases, the bead of mercury rises.

a What does the rising of the mercury bead indicate about the volume of gas in the capillary tube?

b Explain the change in the volume of the gas in terms of the kinetic model of a gas.

14 A small child is taking their first flight and asks a parent if the air is warmer when the plane is flying as it is closer to the Sun. At 35 000 feet, the atmospheric pressure is approximately 24 000 Pa. Use your understanding of pressure and temperature to explain how you would answer the child.

15 Explain why a balloon is more likely to burst if it is sitting on top of a radiator.

16 A student notices that when they pull out the plunger of a sealed syringe to increase the volume of gas in the syringe, the plunger returns to its original position when released.

a As the plunger is pulled out:

 i what happens to the pressure of the gas in the syringe?

 ii how will the air pressure of the gas in the syringe compare to the air pressure of the air in the room?

b Using your answer to part **a**, explain why the plunger returns to its original position when released.

Exercise 9A Wave characteristics

This exercise includes coverage of:
N3 Wave properties
N4 Wave characteristics

1 What is transferred by all types of waves?

2 Give **three** different examples of a wave.

3 State what is meant by these terms used when describing waves:

   a crest   **b** trough   **c** amplitude

   d wavelength   **e** frequency

4 Label this wave with these terms:

crest   **trough**   **amplitude**   **wavelength**

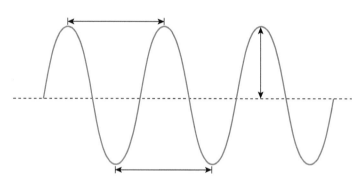

N4   **5** For each of these wave traces, calculate the amplitude of the wave.

a

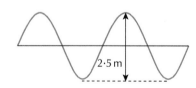

2·5 m

b

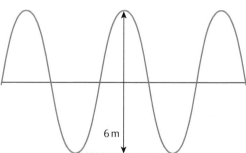

6 m

c

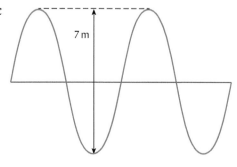

7 m

d

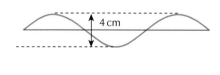

4 cm

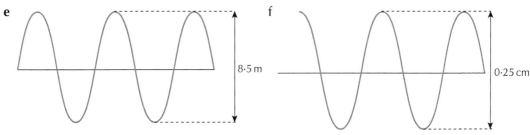
e   8·5 m   f   0·25 cm

N4 **6** Calculate the wavelength for each of these wave traces.

a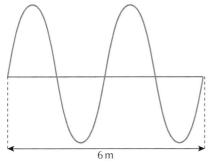
6 m

b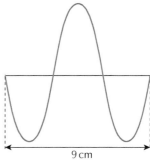
9 cm

c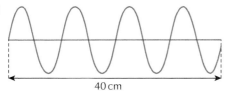
40 cm

d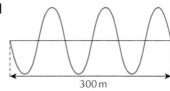
300 m

e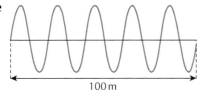
100 m

f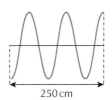
250 cm

N4 **7** The wavelength of this wave is 5 cm. Calculate the distance from A to B.

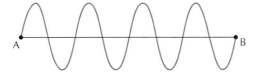
A   B

Exercise 9B Types of waves

This exercise includes coverage of:

N4 Wave characteristics

N4 **1** State what is meant by a **transverse** wave.

N4 **2** Give **two** examples of a transverse wave.

N4 **3** State what is meant by a **longitudinal** wave.

N4 **4** Give **one** example of a longitudinal wave.

N4 **5** **a** What type of wave is shown in this diagram?

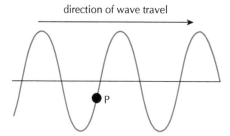

direction of wave travel

P

b The wave is travelling from left to right. Describe the motion of a particle at point P.

N4 **6** **a** What type of wave is shown in this diagram?

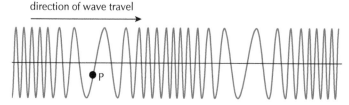

direction of wave travel

P

b The wave in part **a** is travelling from left to right. Describe the motion of a particle at point P.

N4 **7** A teacher wants to show the two different types of waves to their class with a long slinky spring. Write a description of what they could do to show:

a a transverse wave

b a longitudinal wave.

Exercise 9C Frequency, wavelength and speed

This exercise includes coverage of:

N4 Wave characteristics

Example 9.1

A wave has a frequency of 50 000 Hz. The wavelength is $5 \cdot 0 \times 10^{-3}$ m. Calculate the speed of a wave.

frequency = 50 000 Hz

wavelength = $5 \cdot 0 \times 10^{-3}$ m = 0·005 m ●———(Write out what you know from the question.)

speed = frequency × wavelength ●———(Write out the equation (relationship).)

speed = 50 000 × 0·005 ●———(Substitute in what you know.)

speed = 250 m/s ●———(Solve for speed.)

N4 **1** If a pupil knows the number of waves that pass them in a certain time period, how can they calculate the frequency of the wave? State the equation used to calculate the frequency of a wave.

N4 **2** State the units of frequency.

N4 **3** How many hertz are there in 1 kilohertz?

N4 **4** Describe what will happen to the frequency of a wave if the number of waves produced every second is increased.

N4 **5** Calculate the frequency for waves with these characteristics.

    a 20 waves pass a point in 5 seconds.

    b 100 waves pass a point in 25 seconds.

    c 3 waves are produced in 0·5 seconds.

    d 240 waves are generated in 0·12 seconds.

    e 20 000 waves are generated in 0·5 seconds.

    f 2000 waves pass under a bridge in 5 minutes.

N4 **6** A loudspeaker generates 60 000 waves every 5 seconds. Calculate the frequency of the sound.

N4 **7** A pupil plays middle C on the piano. The note has a frequency of 262 Hz. Calculate how many waves are produced if the sound lasts 2 seconds.

N4 **8** A wave machine in a swimming pool has a frequency of 3 Hz. Calculate how many waves are produced in 10 minutes.

N4 **9** Use the relationship

$$v = \text{frequency} \times \text{wavelength, or } v = f\lambda$$

Hint Remember: v represents speed, λ represents wavelength.

to determine the missing values in this table.

Speed (m/s)	Frequency (Hz)	Wavelength (m)
1080	**a**	180
10	**b**	0·25
c	85	4·0
d	10 000	2×10^{-3}
3×10^{8}	$1{\cdot}5 \times 10^{5}$	**e**
250	$1{\cdot}0 \times 10^{7}$	**f**

Hint Large numbers can be represented in scientific notation. $1{\cdot}2 \times 10^{6}$ is a different way of writing 1 200 000. 1×10^{-3} is a different way of writing 0·001.

N4 **10** A sound wave has a frequency of 900 Hz and a wavelength of 0·3 m. Calculate the speed of the wave.

N4 **11** A wave has a wavelength of 10 m and a frequency of 34 Hz. Calculate the speed of the wave.

N4 **12** A light wave travels at 300 000 000 m/s with a wavelength of 0·003 m. Calculate the frequency of the wave.

N4 **13** A water wave has a wavelength of 1·2 m and a speed of 2·4 m/s. Calculate the frequency of the wave.

N4 **14** A sound wave with speed 340 m/s is generated with a frequency of 16 000 Hz. Calculate the wavelength of the wave.

N4 **15** An ultrasound is generated with a frequency of 7 MHz. It travels at 1540 m/s. Calculate the wavelength of the ultrasound wave.

Use the relationship

$$v = \frac{\text{distance}}{\text{time}} = \frac{d}{t}$$

to determine the missing values in this table.

Speed (m/s)	Distance (m)	Time (s)
250	**a**	25
654	**b**	8
c	10 000	7500
d	0·008	0·002
300 000 000	500	**e**
0·04	2	**f**

Light has a speed of 300 000 000 m/s. How far will it travel in:

a 1 second

b 60 seconds

c 1 day?

a Two students carried out an experiment to measure the speed of a wave. They recorded these results:

    10·2 m/s   10·3 m/s   9·2 m/s   10·2 m/s   10·1 m/s

Calculate the average speed of the wave.

b Which result do you think was the anomaly? Explain your answer.

The pupils measured more waves and recorded their results. They used their results to draw this graph.

c State four things that could be done to improve the graph.

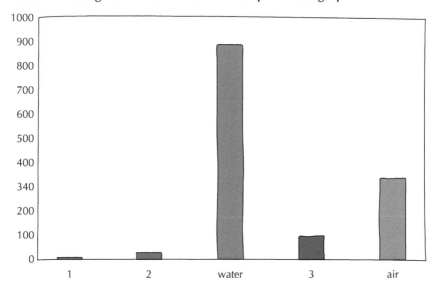

10 Sound

Exercise 10A Sound waves

This exercise includes coverage of:

N3 Sound

CL4 Vibrations and waves SCN 4-11a

1 Use the words provided to copy and complete the following paragraph.

> **wave**   **same**   **sound**   **vibrates**   **collide**

_ _ _ _ _ is a longitudinal wave. The particles in the wave move in the _ _ _ _ direction that the wave is travelling. When something _ _ _ _ _ _ _ _ it sets the particles around it vibrating. These particles _ _ _ _ _ _ _ with other particles. The kinetic energy of these collisions is carried as a sound _ _ _ _.

2 Describe an experiment to show that sound waves are caused by vibrations. Make sure you include:

- what equipment you will need
- what observations you will make
- any safety considerations you should make.

Exercise 10B Human hearing range

This exercise includes coverage of:

N3 Sound

1 Use the table to answer the questions.

Animal	Frequencies they can make (Hz)	Frequencies they can hear (Hz)
Cat	740–1600	60–65 000
Dog	450–1000	15–50 000
Robin	2000–13 000	250–21 000
Human	80–4100	20–20 000
Grasshopper	7000–10 000	100–14 500
Bat	10 000–120 000	1000–120 000

  a Which animal has the widest hearing range?

  b Which animal can produce the lowest frequencies?

  c Which animals hear a wider range of frequencies than humans?

  d A dog whistle has a frequency of 26 000 Hz. Which animals would hear it?

  e Why do you think dog owners use a whistle that they can't hear themselves?

  f Plot a suitable graph of the maximum frequency the animals can hear.

2 What is the range of human hearing?

3 Suggest a reason why the maximum frequency you can hear changes as you get older.

This exercise includes coverage of:

N3 Sound

N4 Sound

1 The diagram shows a wave trace. State the name given to the measurements **X** and **Y**. Pick your answer from the table.

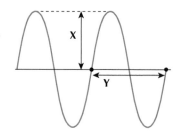

	X is the …	Y is the …
A	trough	wavelength
B	amplitude	frequency
C	amplitude	wavelength
D	wavelength	crest

2 Match each word to its correct meaning.

Word	Meaning
Crest	the number of waves that pass a fixed point per second.
Trough	the height of the wave (from the middle to the top).
Amplitude	the highest point of the wave.
Frequency	the lowest point of the wave.

3 A loud sound is produced by waves with:

A a high pitch   **B** a high frequency

C a small amplitude   **D** a big amplitude.

4 The pitch of a sound is a measure of:

A how loud or quiet it is   **B** how much energy it carries

C how high or low it is   **D** what type of wave it is.

N4 **5** The diagram shows a number of wave traces. Which of the statements on the next page are true? (There is more than one correct answer.)

1

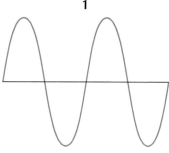

2

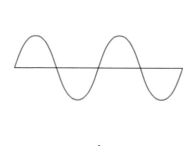

3

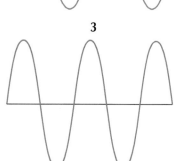

4

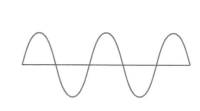

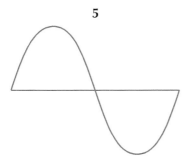

5

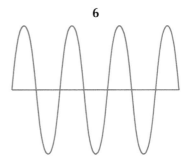

6

A **1** is louder than **2**

B **1** and **3** have the same amplitude

C **1, 3, 5** and **6** all have the same volume

D **4** is louder than **3**

E **6** has a higher frequency than **5**

F **5** has the lowest frequency

G **3** and **6** have the same frequency.

Exercise 10D Measuring the speed of sound

This exercise includes coverage of:

N3 Sound

N4 Sound

 1 Use the words provided to copy and complete the following paragraph. You may need to use the words more than once.

> **liquids**   **wave**   **gases**   **solids**   **light**   **sound**   **vacuum**

Sound can travel through _ _ _ _ _ _, _ _ _ _ _ _ _ _ and _ _ _ _ _. Sound cannot travel through a _ _ _ _ _ _, because there are no particles to allow the _ _ _ _ to travel. Sound travels fastest in _ _ _ _ _ _ because the particles are very close together. _ _ _ _ _ also travels as a wave. _ _ _ _ _ waves are faster than _ _ _ _ _ waves.

2 A pupil sets up the following apparatus to measure the speed of sound in air.

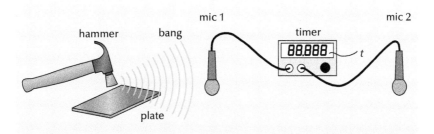

The timer starts when the sound wave reaches microphone 1 and stops when the sound wave reaches microphone 2.

a What else must the pupil measure before finding the speed of sound?

b What piece of apparatus could they use?

c Explain how the pupil could use these measurements to determine the speed of sound in air.

3 Use the relationship

$$v = \frac{d}{t}$$

to determine the missing values in this table.

Speed (m/s)	Distance (m)	Time (s)
340	a	0·1
340	b	0·004
c	1000	3·2
d	1500	4·8
335	500	e
680	68 000	f

N4 **4** The speed of sound in fresh water is 1482 m/s. Calculate the time it takes a sound wave to travel 5000 m in water.

N4 **5** The speed of sound in air is 340 m/s. Calculate the distance travelled by a sound wave in air in 3 seconds.

N4 **6** The speed of sound in pure carbon dioxide is 270 m/s. Calculate the distance travelled by a sound wave in carbon dioxide in 3 seconds.

N4 **7** A person is standing 50 m from a large cliff face. They shout loudly and hear an echo. The speed of sound in air is 340 m/s. Calculate how long it takes for the person to hear the echo.

N4 **8** A seismic survey boat detects an echo from the seafloor 0·3 seconds after it sends out the sound wave. The speed of sound in sea water is 1500 m/s. Calculate the distance to the seafloor.

Exercise 10E Sound level

This exercise includes coverage of:

N3 Sound

1 A student is measuring sound levels in different parts of their school. They record their results in a table.

Place	Sound level (dB)
Quiet classroom	40
Noisy classroom	
The playground during break	70
The busy road outside	80

Suggest a value for the sound level in the noisy classroom.

2 Use the information in this table to help answer the following questions.

Sound level (dB)	Example
0	Threshold of hearing
20	Quiet bedroom
40	Library
50	Ordinary conversation
60	A typical classroom
70	Passenger car, travelling at 35 mph
80	Traffic at a busy roadside
100	Pneumatic drill
120	Threshold of pain
160	Gunfire

a State the two sounds that are above 80 dB.

b What is the sound level of an ordinary conversation?

c Plot a suitable graph of these different noise levels.

3 Suggest **two** things that can be done to reduce your exposure to loud noises.

Exercise 10F Uses of sound

This exercise includes coverage of:

N3 Sound

N4 Sound

CL4 Vibrations and waves SCN 4-11a

1 State what is meant by **ultrasound**.

2 What frequency must a wave have if it is to be described as an **infrasound**?

N4 **3** During an ultrasound scan, a baby's head reflects the ultrasound pulse, which travels at 1500 m/s. The time taken to detect the echo is 5×10^{-5} s. Calculate the distance from the ultrasound scanner to the baby's head.

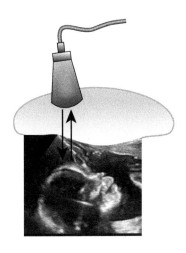

Read the following passage then answer the questions below.

In the early days of sound recording and reproduction, sound was recorded using analogue techniques. Vinyl records and tape recordings used analogue technology.

In the 1980s, sound recording started using digital techniques. Sound waves were recorded and converted into digital electronic signals. This made it easier to change the recorded sounds and add effects. Voices could be altered and music changed.

Recording and reproduction equipment must have an input, a processor and an output. The output is usually a loudspeaker. These can be very large and produce high amplitude waves. Earphones are another type of output device and need to be small enough to fit in your ears so you can listen to your own music.

a Give **two** examples of analogue sound recordings.

b When did sound recording start to use digital techniques?

c What are the advantages of digital recordings?

d What are **three** electronic parts needed for recording and reproducing sound?

Some headphones have noise cancellation technology. Write a description of how this works.

Try to include the terms **signal** and **inverted signal** in your answer.

6 a Use the information in the table to draw a pie chart showing the percentage of sales of music in different formats for 2015.

Format	Percentage (%)
CD	44
Download	35
Subscription and streaming	18
Vinyl	3

b These values were for the year 2015. Make a prediction for the percentage of CD sales for the year 2020. Explain your answer.

11 Light

Exercise 11A Light travels in straight lines

This exercise includes coverage of:

N3 Light

1 Which line in the diagram best represents the light travelling from a candle flame?

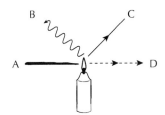

2 Use your understanding of the properties of light rays to explain why we cannot see around corners.

3 A shadow puppet can be created by shining light onto your hands near a wall.

Draw a ray diagram to explain how the shadow puppet is formed.

4 A student investigates how the length of a shadow of a metre stick varies with time of day. Their results are recorded in the table as shown.

Time	Shadow length (m)
9 am	1·50
10 am	1·11
11 am	0·86
12 pm	0·71
1 pm	0·64
2 pm	0·66
3 pm	0·78
4 pm	0·98
5 pm	1·29

a Draw a line graph to show how the length of the shadow varies with time of day.

b When is the length of the shadow shortest?

c When is the length of the shadow longest?

d Predict the length of the shadow at 6 pm. Explain why you predict this value.

5 Copy and complete the diagram by adding rays to show how the position of the Sun in the sky affects the length of the shadows. Use the diagram to help explain the results in the table in Question 4.

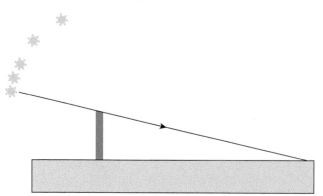

Exercise 11B Reflection of light

This exercise includes coverage of:

N3 Light

1 State the law of reflection.

2 A pupil investigating the law of reflection arranges a ray box with a ray of light incident on a plane mirror. The diagram shows the angles of the incident light.

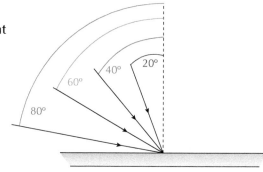

Create a table with two columns headed **Angle of incidence** and **Angle of reflection**. Write in the angles of incidence shown in the diagram in one column and complete the table by writing in the expected values for the matching angles of reflection.

3 This table has been made to explain the meaning of terms associated with reflection of light, but the descriptions do not correctly match the terms. Rewrite the table with the descriptions correctly matching the terms.

Term	Description
Incident ray	The dashed line drawn at right angles to the mirror. Light incident on this line would reflect back along the same path.
Reflected ray	The angle measured between the incident ray and the normal line.
Normal line	The ray of light going to the mirror.
Angle of incidence	The angle measured between the reflected ray and the normal line.
Angle of reflection	The ray of light that comes from the mirror.

4 State the angle of reflection in this diagram.

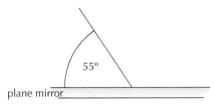

55°

plane mirror

5 **a** State what happens when parallel rays of light are incident on a concave mirror.

b Draw a diagram to illustrate part **a**.

6 **a** State what happens when parallel rays of light are incident on a convex mirror.

b Draw a diagram to illustrate part **a**.

7 State the effect by which light is transmitted along a long glass fibre.

8 Describe **three** uses of optical glass fibres.

Exercise 11C Lenses and refraction of light

This exercise includes coverage of:

N3 Light

N4 Electromagnetic spectrum

CL3 Forces, electricity and waves SCN 3-11a

1 When light travels from air to glass, the light can change direction.

a State the name of this effect.

b State another change that happens to the light when it travels from air to glass.

2 A ray of light strikes a glass object placed under a cover.
The ray diagram shows how the ray exits the glass object.

a Which of these glass objects is under the cover?

A   B   C   D   E

b Draw a diagram to show how the ray of light passes through the object you have selected in part **a**.

3 The diagram shows what happens to a ray of light when it enters a semi-circular glass block.

Copy and complete the diagram by marking:

a the angle of incidence

b the angle of refraction

c the normal line.

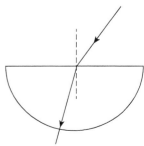

4 What effect does a convex lens have on parallel rays passing through it? You may draw a diagram to aid your explanation.

5 What effect does a concave lens have on parallel rays passing through it? You may draw a diagram to aid your explanation.

N4 **6** A family are out for a drive in the countryside. The father, driving the car, needs glasses to see clearly the number plates of the cars ahead. A grandfather, sitting in the passenger seat, can see the number plates fine, but needs glasses to see the map. In the back seat, a child can see both the number plates of the cars in front and the magazine they are reading.

a Copy and complete the diagrams below to show how the light focuses on the retina of the child when looking at a distant object (at the cars in front) and a near object (at their magazine).

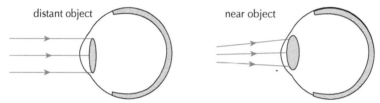

distant object   near object

b The father is short-sighted.

   i Copy the diagram of the eye above for the distant object, and complete the diagram to show how the rays are focused by the lens in the eye for the father, if he was not wearing glasses.

   ii State what type of lens is used in his glasses to see the cars in front clearly.

c The grandfather is long-sighted.

   i Copy the diagram of the eye above for the near object, and complete the diagram to show how the rays are focused by the lens in the eye for the grandfather, if he was not wearing glasses.

   ii State what type of lens is used in his glasses to enable him to see the map clearly.

Exercise 11D Colour

This exercise includes coverage of:

N3 Colour

1 The diagram shows what happens when white light passes through a prism.

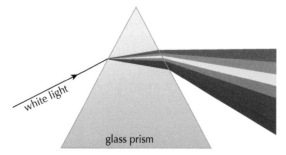

white light

glass prism

a State the name given to the range of colours produced by the prism.

b Explain why the white light produces different colours of light when it passes through the prism.

2 State the **three** primary colours of light.

3 When the primary colours are mixed, new colours are produced, as shown in the diagram.

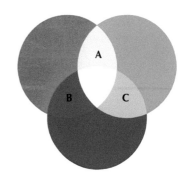

   a State the name given to the colours produced when the primary colours are mixed.

   b For each of the colours labelled **A**, **B** and **C** in the diagram:

      i state the name of the colour

      ii state which primary colours are mixed together to produce it.

   c What colour is produced when all three primary colours are mixed together?

4 White light is shone onto a white t-shirt. Which colours contained in the white light are reflected?

5 White light is shone onto a matt black jacket. Which colours contained in the white light are reflected?

6 White light is shone onto a blue plate. State which colours are absorbed by the plate and which colours are reflected.

7 White light is shone onto a pink lunchbox. Explain why it appears pink.

8 Blue light is shone onto a ripe yellow banana. Explain why it appears black.

9 State the name of the condition that affects a person's ability to see colour correctly.

Exercise 11E Optical instruments

This exercise includes coverage of:

N3 Optical instruments

CL3 Forces, electricity and waves SCN 3-11a

1 A periscope uses mirrors to see around obstacles.

   a How many mirrors are needed for a periscope to operate correctly?

   b Light is incident on one of the mirrors in a periscope at an angle of 45°. What is the angle of reflection?

2 An aspiring young astronomer uses a refracting telescope to look at the Moon. The diagram shows the outline of the telescope, but the lenses at positions **A** and **B** have been left out.

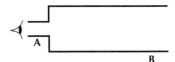

   a Complete the diagram by drawing the two lenses in their correct positions.

   b By drawing incoming parallel rays, show what happens to the incoming light from the Moon.

   c State the name and purpose of the lens at:

      i position **A**   **ii** position **B**.

3 A pinhole camera is directed at a candle. Two rays show how an image of the candle is formed by the pinhole camera.

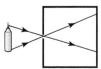

The camera is then moved farther away from the candle.

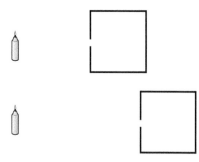

a Draw two rays from each candle to show how the image is formed by the pinhole camera when the camera is farther away from the candle.

b What do the diagrams indicate happens to the image produced by a pinhole camera when it moves farther away from the object it is capturing?

c State **two** differences between a pinhole camera and a modern optical camera.

4 A periscope is designed so that the top mirror can be rotated. This lets the user see behind them. The diagram shows a simplified view of the periscope with the top mirror facing backwards.

Two rays of light reflecting off a person standing at a distance enter the periscope as shown.

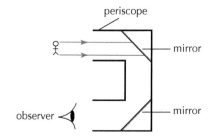

a Complete the diagram to show the path of the two rays leaving the periscope.

b Describe what is unusual about the image the observer can see using the periscope in this way.

c By using the rays you have drawn for part **a**, or otherwise, explain the image seen by the observer.

12 EM spectrum

Exercise 12A The electromagnetic spectrum

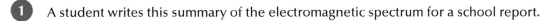

This exercise includes coverage of:

N3 Electromagnetic radiation

N4 Electromagnetic spectrum

CL3 Vibrations and waves SCN 3-11b

CL4 Vibrations and waves SCN 4-11b

1 A student writes this summary of the electromagnetic spectrum for a school report.

The electromagnetic spectrum is a range of radiations, each having different wavelengths, and speeds. The frequency of all types of radiation is the same. Radio waves carry sound information, so travel at the speed of sound. The only types of electromagnetic radiation that humans can see is UV and visible light. Since the electromagnetic spectrum is made of radiation, exposure to it can be dangerous.

Use your knowledge of physics to answer the questions below relating to the paragraph.

a Comment on the student's understanding of these properties of the electromagnetic spectrum:

   i frequency   **ii** wavelength   **iii** speed.

b Is the student correct in their understanding of which parts of the EM spectrum humans can see? Explain your answer.

c Comment on the truth, or otherwise, of the closing sentence of the student's paragraph.

2 Gamma radiation is used in radiotherapy to treat cancer.

a State the effect that gamma radiation has on cancer cells.

b Sources of gamma radiation can be injected into the body to diagnose illness. The gamma rays pass through the body and are detected outside the body.

   i What is the term used to describe gamma radiation when used to diagnose illness?

   ii State how the gamma radiation can be detected outside the body.

c State **two** other uses of gamma radiation.

3 X-rays can be used for viewing inside the body.

a State **one** type of material in the body that X-rays can easily pass through.

b State **one** type of material in the body that X-rays cannot pass through.

c What is used to detect X-rays that have passed through the body?

d State **two** safety precautions that radiographers must use when administering X-rays to patients.

4 State **two** uses for X-rays, other than for seeing inside the body.

5 Two friends are having an argument about the dangers of being in sunlight. One says *'We should never go outside without suntan lotion, as the sun is harmful for our skin'.* The other says they never use suntan lotion because sunlight is good for us. Use your knowledge of physics to comment on the accuracy of each person's claims.

6 Describe **one** application of UV light.

7 Visible light is the only part of the electromagnetic spectrum visible to the human eye. How else can visible light be detected?

8 All hot objects emit infrared radiation.

    a State the speed of infrared radiation.

    b What can be used to detect infrared radiation?

    c Describe what a thermogram is.

    d State **one** medical use of infrared radiation.

    e State **one** way in which infrared radiation has changed our way of life.

9 Microwaves are used in microwave ovens to heat food.

    a Explain how microwaves can be used to heat food.

    b How does the frequency of microwave radiation compare with infrared radiation?

    c State **one** other use for microwaves.

    d State how microwaves can be detected.

N4 **10** This diagram of the electromagnetic spectrum is found on a science education website. The only parts identified are X-rays and microwaves.

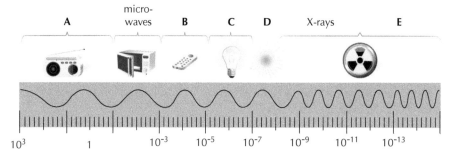

    a Identify the five regions of the electromagnetic spectrum missing from the diagram, labelled **A**, **B**, **C**, **D** and **E**.

    b State what the numbers along the bottom of the diagram represent. Explain the reason for your answer.

    c In which region of the spectrum do the waves have the shortest wavelength?

    d Describe what happens to the frequency of the waves in the electromagnetic spectrum as the wavelength decreases.

    e In which region of the spectrum do the waves have the lowest frequency?

    f An electromagnetic wave has a wavelength of 10^{-9} metres. What type of wave is it?

N4 **11** State which part of the electromagnetic spectrum has wavelengths more than 1 km.

12 A physics student creates this poster showing different parts of the electromagnetic spectrum.

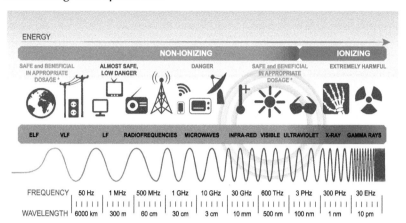

With reference to the diagram above, answer the following questions.

a Which parts of the EM spectrum are classed as ionising?

b Although microwave radiation is non-ionising, state why you think the student has added the label **DANGER** to this form of EM radiation?

c Explain why the student has chosen the diagram above the term **INFRA-RED**.

At the bottom of the diagram, the student has shown the wavelength of each type of EM radiation.

d i What does the prefix **k** stand for in the value **6000 km**.

ii What does the prefix **m** stand for in the value **10 mm**.

The student has added frequency values for the radiations.

e i Estimate a value of the frequency of a TV signal.

ii What does the prefix **M** stand for in the value **1 MHz**?

iii What does the prefix **G** stand for in the value **10 GHz**?

N4 **13** State whether the statements below are true or false.

a Gamma rays travel faster than X-rays.

b Radio waves transmit TV signals as well as radio signals.

c TV remote controls use UV to communicate with the television.

d Overexposure to X-rays can be dangerous.

e Gamma rays can be detected with a Geiger–Müller tube counter.

f Light travels at 340 m/s.

g Humans can only see a tiny portion of the entire electromagnetic spectrum.

N4 **14** By referring to the positive impact that our understanding of the EM spectrum has had on society, write a short paragraph (100 words or less) in support of continued investment in scientific research.

13 Nuclear radiation

Exercise 13A Atoms and radiation

N4 **1** Label the different parts of the diagram.

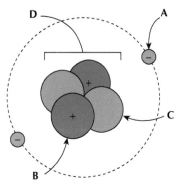

This table shows some properties of different types of radiation.

Name	What it is	How far it travels in air	Absorbed by	Speed of travel	Ionising effect
Alpha	Two protons and two neutrons from the nucleus	Around 8 cm	Paper	Slow (15×10^6 m/s)	Strong
Beta	An electron emitted from the nucleus due to the decay process	Around 1 m	Thin sheet of aluminium	Fast (270×10^6 m/s)	Weak
Gamma	A wave of energy, part of the electromagnetic spectrum	Very far (can be up to 100s of metres in air)	Several metres of lead	The speed of light (300×10^6 m/s)	Very weak

Use the information in the table to answer these questions.

N4 **2** Name the **three** types of radiation.

N4 **3** Explain what is meant by an alpha particle.

N4 **4** How far can gamma radiation travel in air?

N4 **5** What material can beta radiation be absorbed by?

N4 **6** Write the three types of radiation in order of decreasing ionising effect.

N4 **7** A teacher demonstrates the effect of different materials in absorbing different types of radiation received from a radioactive source.

material being investigated

source

counter

The results are recorded in the table.

Material being investigated	Amount of radiation received (corrected counts)
Air	1753
Tissue paper	321
Aluminium foil	1
Lead sheet	0

a Which material absorbed the most radiation?

b Which of the three types of radiation do you think was used in the experiment? Explain your answer.

N4 **8** Choose the correct letter to complete the sentence.

Background radiation is:

A only found in a few places

B only caused by natural sources

C not common

D found all around us.

N4 **9** Choose the correct letter to complete the sentence.

Background nuclear radiation can come from:

A radon gas in the atmosphere

B mobile phones

C microwaves

D computer games.

N4 **10** Choose the correct letter to complete the sentence.

Background radiation:

A causes significant health risks

B causes cancer

C does not harm humans at the normal level

D is the same everywhere on the Earth.

N4 **11** List **three** examples of natural radiation and **three** examples of man-made radiation.

N4 **12** List **three** safety precautions needed when handling radioactive sources.

Read the following passage then answer the questions.

A film badge is used to measure the levels of radiation that a person is exposed to. Film badges use photographic film. This film turns white when exposed to radiation. After the film has been used, it is developed and analysed to show the type and level of radiation the badge has been exposed to. If the film behind the lead window has turned white the person who was wearing the badge must have been exposed to gamma radiation.

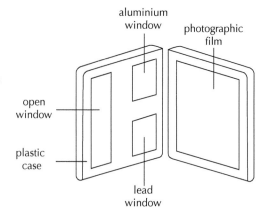

a What type of film is placed inside the badge?

b What colour does this film go if exposed to radiation?

c What type of radiation has the person been exposed to if the film behind the lead window is white when the film is developed?

d Use your knowledge of radiation to state what type of radiation the person has been exposed to if only the film behind the open window is white when the film is developed.

Exercise 13B Uses of radiation

This exercise includes coverage of:

N4 Nuclear radiation

CL3 Vibrations and waves SCN 3-11b

CL4 Vibrations and waves SCN 4-11b

N4 (1) The diagram shows equipment used for measuring the thickness of paper. Describe how a radioactive source can be used in this equipment.

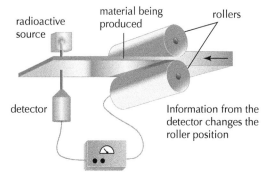

N4 (2) Why is beta radiation better than alpha radiation when measuring the thickness of paper?

N4 (3) Describe how a radioactive source can be used as a tracer to detect medical issues in the body.

N4 (4) Why is gamma radiation better than alpha radiation when using radioactive tracers in medicine?

This exercise includes coverage of:

N4 Nuclear radiation

CL4 Energy sources and sustainability SCN 4-04a; Topical science SCN 4-20b

N4 **1** Create a table of the advantages and disadvantages of nuclear power. Sort these sentences into your table.

> Nuclear power plants do not need a lot of space.
>
> Decommissioning of nuclear power stations is expensive and takes a long time.
>
> Nuclear accidents can spread radiation over large distances and harm many lives.
>
> Nuclear power plants have to be built near a large body of water for cooling purposes.
>
> Nuclear power stations do not contribute to carbon emissions.
>
> Nuclear power stations do not produce smoke particles that contribute to acid rain.
>
> A lot of energy is produced from a small mass of fuel.
>
> Nuclear power does not depend on the weather.
>
> Disposal of nuclear waste is very expensive.

N4 **2** Why does some radioactive waste need to be stored securely for a long period of time?

3 Write a 100-word paragraph explaining if you would or would not like a nuclear power station built near your house.

4 Even though there are strict safety procedures nuclear accidents can happen. The cooling systems in the Fukushima nuclear power plant were damaged after an earthquake and tsunami. Without the cooling systems, the reactors overheated. This caused a radiation leak. Around 160 000 people were evacuated from their homes and there is still a no-go area around the site.

Use your knowledge of physics to comment on this information.

14 Speed and acceleration

Exercise 14A Speed, distance and time

1 What is meant by the term **speed**?

2 Which of the following could be units for speed?

A newtons	**B** metres per second
C miles per hour	**D** seconds
E m/s	**F** kilometres per hour
G volts	

3 The table shows typical speeds for everyday activities.

Object	Speed (m/s)
Person walking	1·2
Person running	
Person cycling	8·9
Bus	13·4
Car	17·9

Suggest a value for the speed of a person running.

4 A car travelling at 20 mph covers 20 miles in 1 hour. What do the following measurements mean?

> **Hint** Write out the measurement in words.

a 60 mph   **b** 13 m/s   **c** 40 km/h

N4 **5** Use the relationship

$$v = \frac{\text{distance}}{\text{time}} = \frac{d}{t}$$

> **Hint** Remember v is used to represent speed.

to calculate the missing values in the table.

Distance (m)	Time (s)	Speed (m/s)
100	5	**a**
0·35	0·50	**b**
12 000	**c**	24
45	**d**	0·75
e	60	8·9
f	360	6·2

N4 **6** Calculate these speeds.

   a A man runs 100 m in 10 s.

   b A car travels 60 m in 5 s.

   c A plane flies 1 000 000 m in 11 200 s.

   d A snail moves 0·5 m in 250 s.

   e Put the objects in parts **a–d** in order of speed from slowest to fastest.

N4 **7** A cyclist cycles for 3 hours at an average speed of 20 km/h. Calculate how far she travels.

N4 **8** A slug moves at a speed of 0·09 m/s. Calculate how long it will take to cover a distance of 1·8 m.

N4 **9** A runner completes a 200 m race in 24 s. Calculate their average speed.

N4 **10** The speed of sound varies with altitude. The supersonic plane Concorde cruised at an altitude of 18 000 m. At this altitude, the speed of sound is 295 m/s. Concorde cruised at twice the speed of sound. Calculate how far Concorde would have cruised in 3 hours.

> **Hint** Remember there are 3600 seconds in 1 hour.

Exercise 14B Average and instantaneous speed

This exercise includes coverage of:

N4 Speed and acceleration

N4 **1** State what is meant by the term **average speed**.

N4 **2** Give an example of a situation where average speed is measured.

N4 **3** State what is meant by the term **instantaneous speed**.

N4 **4** Give an example of a situation where instantaneous speed is measured.

N4 **5** Describe how to measure the average speed of a toy car on a ramp. Your description should include:

   • what equipment you need

   • a diagram to show how the equipment is arranged

   • the measurements that you make

   • any equations you use.

N4 **6** Describe how to measure the instantaneous speed of a toy car on a ramp. Your description should include:

   • what equipment you need

   • a diagram to show how the equipment is arranged

   • the measurements that you make

   • any equations you use.

N4 **7** The police use both average and instantaneous speed cameras on the roads to check the speed of vehicles. Which type of speed camera is most effective in reducing road accidents? Explain your answer.

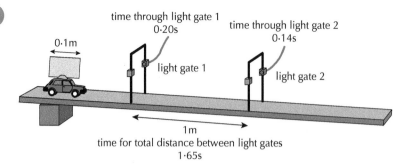

a Calculate the instantaneous speed through light gate 1.

b Calculate the instantaneous speed through light gate 2.

c Calculate the average speed for the full distance.

Drivers have to be aware of their speeds when driving on roads. The faster the car is travelling the longer it will take to stop. The Highway Code has information about the distances a car will travel as it slows down.

Speed (mph)	Thinking distance (m)	Braking distance (m)	Total stopping distance (m) (thinking + braking)
20	6	6	
30	9	14	
40	12	24	
50	15	38	
60	18	55	
70	21	75	

a Calculate the total braking distance for each speed to complete the last column.

b Suggest **one** factor that could affect a person's thinking time.

c Suggest **one** factor that could affect a car's braking distance.

d Plot a line graph to show the information in the table.

> Hint | For this graph, speed should be on the vertical axis and distance on the horizontal axis. Use different colours for each category of distance and make a key so it is clear which line is which.

e Use your graph to suggest a value for the thinking distance at 35 mph.

f Use your graph to suggest a value for the braking distance at 45 mph.

g Use your graph to suggest a value for the total stopping distance at 55 mph.

This exercise includes coverage of:

N4 Speed and acceleration

CL4 Forces SCN 4-07a

N4 **1** Describe the motion represented in these speed–time graphs.

a
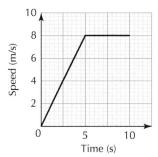

b
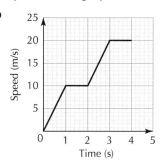

c
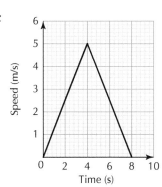

d
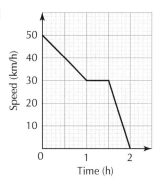

N4 **2** Plot a speed–time graph for each of these data sets.

a

Time (s)	0	1	2	3	4
Speed (m/s)	0	7	7	7	7

b

Time (s)	0	5	10	15	20
Speed (m/s)	20	15	15	10	5

c

Time (h)	0	1	2	3	4
Speed (km/h)	100	125	150	150	200

d

Time (days)	0	1	2	3	4
Speed (cm/day)	0·01	0·02	0·01	0·05	0·06

e

Time (s)	0	60	120	180	210
Speed (m/s)	10	20	20	30	30

f

Time (s)	0·01	0·05	0·08	0·09	0·13
Speed (m/s)	1	1	2	2	2

N4 **3** For each of these speed–time graphs, find the total distance travelled by calculating the area under the line.

a
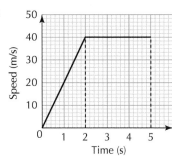

b
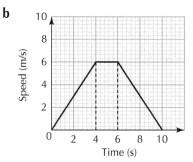

c
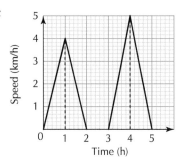

d
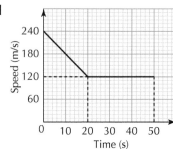

Exercise 14D Acceleration

This exercise includes coverage of:

N4 Speed and acceleration

CL4 Forces SCN 4-07b

N4 **1** State what is meant by the term **acceleration**.

N4 **2** What are the standard units of acceleration?

N4 **3**

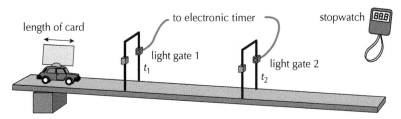

A trolley is released from rest and moves towards the two light gates. The time taken to travel between the light gates is measured with the stopwatch.

a Explain how to calculate acceleration.

b State what would happen to the value of acceleration if the ramp was made steeper.

Use the relationship

$$a = \frac{\Delta v}{t}$$

> **Hint** a represents acceleration, Δv represents change in speed.

to calculate the missing values in the table.

Acceleration (m/s²)	Change in speed (m/s)	Time (s)
a	12	2
b	24	6
c	100	50
d	0·3	0·1
0·4	e	12
0·05	20	f

A car starts from rest and accelerates to 14 m/s in 20 seconds. Calculate the acceleration.

The speed of a train increases from 10 m/s to 25 m/s in 5 seconds. Calculate the acceleration of the train.

A cyclist travels at 8 m/s. He decelerates at 2 m/s² before stopping. Calculate the time he takes to come to a rest.

A lorry travels at 14 m/s and brakes to a stop, decelerating at 0·5 m/s². Calculate the time it takes to come to a rest.

9 Calculate the accelerations for an object that accelerates from

a   2 m/s to 8 m/s in 4 seconds

b   8 m/s to 2 m/s in 4 seconds

c   0 m/s to 30 m/s in 3 seconds

d   10 m/s to 0 m/s in 0·25 seconds.

10 Cars are often ranked on how quickly they can accelerate from 0 mph to 60 mph. These values can be converted into metres per second.

Calculate the acceleration for these cars.

Car	Change in speed (m/s)	Time taken (seconds)	Acceleration (m/s²)
Audi A1 1·0 TFSI SE	26·8	10·7	a
BMW 123d Coupe M-Sport	26·8	6·9	b
Citroen Berlingo e-HDI 90	26·8	14·1	c
Ferrari 458 Spider	26·8	3·3	d
Land Rover Discovery SDV6	26·8	8·7	e
Noble M600	26·8	2·9	f

15 Forces, motion and energy

Exercise 15A Forces

This exercise includes coverage of:

N3 Forces

1. What **three** things can forces do to an object?

2. What piece of apparatus is used to measure forces?

3. What are the units of force?

4. Determine the size of force for each of these meters.

5. For each of these situations, name the forces and the direction in which they are acting. You might need some of these words:

upwards	weight	magnetic	air resistance	electrostatic	pull
force	push	buoyancy	friction	downwards	reaction force

a

person standing on scales

b

north and south pole of magnets

c

dropping a tennis ball

d

rubbing a balloon and sticking it to a wall

e

rubber duck floating in a bath

f

person ice skating

6 A pupil sets up an experiment to find out the force acting on different objects. The objects are attached to a Newton balance and the results are recorded in a table. Each measurement is repeated three times.

Object	Force (N)			Average force (N)
Keys	0·5	0·6	0·4	
Mug	2·3	2·3	2·3	
School bag	8·9	9·1	8·7	
Shoe	3·6	**X**	3·4	
Pencil case	0·9	0·9	1·8	

a Suggest a value for the missing force **X**, acting on the shoe.

b Calculate the average force for each object, including your suggested value.

c Which value for the pencil case do you think was an anomaly?

d Suggest an improvement for this experiment that would make the results more reliable.

Exercise 15B Measuring forces to keep us safe

This exercise includes coverage of:

CL4 Forces SCN 4-07b

1 Read the information, then answer the following questions.

If a car crashes at 30 mph, the driver and any passengers in the car will keep moving at 30 mph until a force acts on them. Without seatbelts providing a force, the people will hit the parts of the car immediately in front of them. 98% of car drivers were recorded wearing a seatbelt in 2014. Drivers and passengers who fail to wear seatbelts in the front and back of vehicles are breaking the law. Drivers caught without a seatbelt face on-the-spot fines of £100.

Car designers make a strong rigid passenger section to keep the people safe. In front and behind this section the car is easily crushed. The parts of the car which are easily crushed are called *crumple zones*. These are manufactured to bend and buckle so that the energy from the collision and the forces involved do not transfer to the people in the car.

a What provides the force stopping people hitting the inside of the car when it crashes?

b What percentage of drivers failed to wear their seatbelts in 2014?

c What are the easily crushed sections of a car called?

d Name **one** other safety feature of cars. Explain how it keeps the people safe. Try to use the word **force** in your answer.

Exercise 15C Balanced forces

1 Explain what is meant by the term **friction**.

2 Give **three** ways to reduce the force of friction acting between two objects.

3 In which of the following situations is friction helpful?

    A a squeaky, rusty door hinge

    B the disc brakes on a bike

    C the thick tread on mountain bike tyres

    D the thin blade on an ice skate

    E the cushion of air on a hovercraft

    F the streamlined swimsuit of an Olympic swimmer

    G the material of a goalkeeper's glove

    H the striking of a match.

4 **a** Skydivers use parachutes to help them land safely. What force increases when the parachute is opened?

    b Explain why this helps the skydiver to slow down.

N4 **5** What happens to the temperature of objects when frictional forces are acting?

N4 **6** State what is meant by the term **balanced forces**.

N4 **7** A van is trying to pull another car out of a muddy ditch. Neither vehicle is moving. What can be said about the size and direction of the forces?

N4 **8** A cyclist travels at steady speed. What can be said about the size and direction of the forces acting on the cyclist?

N4 **9** A car accelerates until it reaches its top speed. What can be said about the size and direction of the forces:

    a while the car is accelerating

    b when it is travelling at full speed?

N4 **10** State the size and direction of the unbalanced force in each diagram.

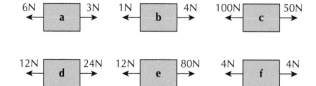

This exercise includes coverage of:

N4 Relationship between forces, motion and energy

CL4 Forces SCN 4-07b

N4 **1** Which of the following statements are true?

A When an unbalanced force acts on an object, the object will continue to move at the same speed.

B If an unbalanced force acts on a small object, it will cause a smaller acceleration than if the same force was applied to a big object.

C Unbalanced forces cause acceleration.

D Two forces that act in the same direction could cause an unbalanced force.

E Two forces that are equal in size but opposite in direction will cause an unbalanced force.

N4 **2** **a** Which of these cars will accelerate?

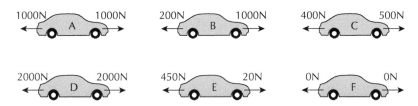

b All the cars have the same mass. Which one will have the greatest acceleration? Explain your answer.

N4 **3** Use the relationship

$$F = ma$$

to calculate the missing values in the table.

Force (N)	Mass (kg)	Acceleration (m/s²)
a	100	0·5
b	0·36	0·22
c	10 000	0·6
254	d	0·04
25 500	e	50
30	900	f
0·23	0·23	g

N4 **4** Calculate the force acting on a ball of mass 0·04 kg when it accelerates at 120 m/s².

N4 **5** Calculate the force acting on a bus of mass 4500 kg when it accelerates at 0·4 m/s².

N4 **6** Calculate the mass of a ship accelerating at 0·32 m/s² if there is an unbalanced force of 10 000 000 N.

N4 **7** The driving force acting on a car is 2500 N. There is a frictional force of 1200 N. Calculate the mass of a car when it is accelerating at 4·0 m/s².

Exercise 15E The force of gravity

1 Explain what is meant by the term **mass**.

2 State the units of mass.

3 What piece of apparatus is used to measure mass?

N4 **4** Explain what is meant by the term **weight**.

N4 **5** State the units of weight.

N4 **6** What piece of apparatus is used to measure weight?

N4 **7** What is the value of the gravitational field strength on Earth?

N4 **8** Use the relationship

$$W = mg$$

> **Hint** g is the gravitational field strength.

to calculate the missing values in the table.

Weight (N)	Mass (kg)	Gravitational field strength (N/kg)
a	55	9·8
b	0·045	9·8
c	0·045	1·6
2405	**d**	3·7
0·20	**e**	9·8
603	67	**f**
116160	10560	**g**

N4 **9** Which statement is not true?

    A The Earth attracts objects because it is moving through space.

    B Large objects always have a large gravitational field strength.

    C All objects are attracted to each other by the force of gravity.

    D The size of the force of gravity depends on the mass of the objects.

N4 **10** The force of gravity is less on the Moon than on the Earth because:

    A the Moon is smaller than the Earth

    B the Moon has a bigger mass than the Earth

    C the Moon is bigger than the Earth

    D the Moon has a smaller mass than the Earth.

16 Satellites

Exercise 16A Satellite orbits

This exercise includes coverage of:

N4 Satellites

N4 **1**   **a** State what is meant by a **natural satellite**.

     b Give **two** examples of natural satellites in our Solar System.

N4 **2**   The table contains data about the orbits of the first four planets in the Solar System nearest to the Sun.

Planet	Distance from Sun (km)	Period of orbit (days)
Mercury	57 900	88
Venus	108 000	225
Earth	150 000	365
Mars	228 000	687

     a Use the values in the table to describe how the period of orbit is affected by the distance between the Sun and the planet.

     b Draw a graph to represent this data.

> **Hint**   Think about the type of graph which would be most suitable and what should go on each axis.

     c Compare the shape of your graph to your answer for part **a**. Explain how the graph confirms, or otherwise, your answer for part **a**.

N4 **3**   A reconnaissance satellite is orbiting the Earth at a height of 450 km above the surface of the Earth.

     a State the name given to satellites that orbit at this height.

     b Describe **one** other application of satellites orbiting at this height, not used for reconnaissance.

N4 **4**   Polar orbiting satellites always pass over the North and South Poles.

     a State how long it takes a polar orbiting satellite to orbit the Earth.

     b State **two** applications of polar orbiting satellites.

     c Explain how a polar orbiting satellite can see the entire surface of the Earth in one day.

N4 **5**   The International Space Station (ISS) takes approximately 90 minutes to orbit the Earth.

     a State whether the ISS is in a low Earth orbit or a medium Earth orbit.

     b Calculate how many times the ISS will orbit the Earth in one day.

     c Describe the purpose of the ISS.

N4 **6**   GPS satellites orbit in medium Earth orbits.

     a State the approximate height above the Earth's surface that GPS satellites will orbit.

     b What does GPS stand for?

 Describe what is meant by a geostationary satellite.

 What is the period of orbit of a geostationary satellite?

 At what height above the Earth's surface do geostationary satellites orbit?

N4 10 The table gives information about four satellites **A**, **B**, **C** and **D** orbiting the Earth. The height of satellite **B** is missing from the table.

Satellite	Height above the Earth's surface	Orbit time
A	300 km	90 minutes
B		2 hours 20 minutes
C	20 000 km	12 hours
D	36 000 km	24 hours

  a Which of the following is a likely height for satellite **B** to orbit the Earth?

    i 250 km   **ii** 2800 km   **iii** 15 000 km   **iv** 60 000 km

  b Which satellite orbits over the North Pole many times in one day?

  c Which satellite remains in a fixed location in the sky?

N4 11 Two friends are looking up at the sky and see a white star-like object moving fairly quickly across the sky. One of the friends says that he thinks it is the International Space Station. The other friend says that it is actually the Sky TV orbiting satellite. State which of the two friends is most likely to be correct and explain your reasoning.

12 On February 6, 2018, the Falcon Heavy rocket launched into space, placing a Tesla Roadster car in orbit around the Sun. The car is now an artificial satellite in orbit around the Sun.

Many astronomers and commentators have complained that launching this car into space has contributed to what is known as space junk.

Using your knowledge of physics, explain what the term space junk means, and explain whether you think this car poses a danger to future missions in space.

Exercise 16B Communicating with satellites

This exercise includes coverage of:

N4 Satellites

N4 1 Some orbiting satellites transmit information between themselves and the ground using radio waves.

  a State **one** other type of wave that is used to transmit information between satellites.

  b State the speed of all wave communication between satellites.

Calculate the time taken for a radio wave signal to travel from a transmitter on the surface of the Earth to these orbiting satellites:

> **Hint** Remember to convert heights to metres before substituting them into the formula.

a an environmental observation satellite orbiting at 250 km above the ground

b a GPS satellite orbiting at 20 500 km

c the International Space Station, orbiting at 408 km

d a weather monitoring satellite orbiting at 35 800 km

e the Hubble Space Telescope, orbiting at 568 km.

News broadcasts are transmitted live across the globe using satellite communication. A news broadcaster uses a geostationary satellite to transmit a signal from New York to London. The geostationary satellite is 35 800 km above both New York and London. The TV signals are carried by microwaves.

a Determine the time taken for the TV signal to travel from New York to London, via the geostationary satellite.

The news broadcaster wants to explore the use of fibre optic cables to send the broadcasts, to see if they would reduce the time taken to send the signal. They use a 6000 km fibre optic cable connecting the two cities to send the signal. The signal in the fibre optic cable is transmitted at 200 000 000 m/s.

b Determine the time taken for the TV signal to be transmitted through the fibre optic cable from New York to London.

c Based on your answers to parts **a** and **b**, state and explain which method of communication would reduce the delay in the transmitted signal.

Radio signals can be transmitted around the world from ground based satellites by bouncing the radio signals off a layer of the atmosphere called the ionosphere.

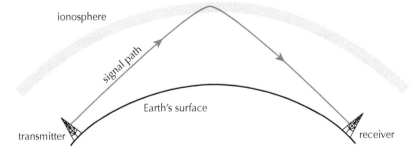

A radio wave signal is sent from a transmitter at one point on the Earth and detected by a receiver at another point on the Earth. The signal takes 0·04 s to travel from the transmitter to the receiver.

a State how long it takes for the signal to travel from the transmitter to the ionosphere.

b Determine the distance that the signal travels between the transmitter and the ionosphere.

N4 **5** The Mars Odyssey is a space probe currently orbiting Mars. It studies the planet's geology and looks for evidence of water and ice.

a Light signals from Mars take 0·013 s to travel from the surface of Mars to the probe. Calculate the height, in km, that the Mars Odyssey is orbiting above the surface of Mars.

> **Hint** Light signals travel at the same speed as radio waves.

b Data collected from the space probe is transmitted back to Earth periodically. It takes the radio signal 182 s to travel from the Mars Odyssey back to Earth. Use this information to determine the approximate distance, in km, between Earth and Mars.

N4 **6** Curved reflectors are used in orbiting satellites.

a State the purpose of a curved reflector on a satellite dish.

b Explain how a curved reflector is used to strengthen incoming signal. You should use a labelled diagram to aid your explanation.

N4 **7** **a** Draw a diagram to show how a curved reflector can be used with a transmitting aerial to produce a parallel beam.

b Explain why some transmitters use curved reflectors to transmit a signal and other transmitters do not.

Exercise 16C Uses of satellites

This exercise includes coverage of:

N4 Satellites

N4 **1** State **three** uses of satellites orbiting the Earth.

N4 **2** Describe **two** ways in which life has been improved by the increased use of telecommunications satellites.

N4 **3** Search online to research how satellites are used in global positioning systems. Your research should cover the following points:

a The history and development of the GPS system designed in the USA.

b A basic explanation of how GPS uses satellites to locate your position.

c Applications of GPS in different areas (e.g., recreation, military, agriculture etc.).

d Future developments of GPS by other nations.

N4 **4** Describe **three** ways in which satellites can be used for military observation.

N4 **5** Describe how weather monitoring satellites use infrared radiation to provide weather information.

N4 **6** Polar orbiting satellites are often used for environmental monitoring.

a State what is meant by environmental monitoring.

b Describe what types of information environmental monitoring satellites can provide about the planet.

N4 **7** Imagine you are in the debating society at your school, and the motion for the next debate is entitled:

> This house believes that satellites have had no positive contribution to society whatsoever.

Use your knowledge of physics to write a 100-word statement to oppose this motion.

17 Planet Earth and the Solar System

Exercise 17A Our planet Earth

This exercise includes coverage of:

N3 Solar System

  Label the diagram showing the different layers in the Earth's structure.

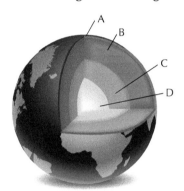

  Read the following information and then answer the following questions.

> The crust is the outermost layer of the Earth. It is rocky and thin compared to the other layers and has an average temperature of 22 °C. The mantle is the thickest layer. It is made up of semi-molten rock called magma. Below the mantle is the outer core. This is a liquid layer of molten iron and nickel. It flows around the inner core and causes the Earth's magnetic field. At the centre of the Earth is the inner core. It is a solid ball of iron and nickel with a temperature of between 5000 °C and 6000 °C.

a Name the four layers of the Earth's structure described in the information, in order from the centre outwards.

b Which is the thinnest layer of the Earth?

c What do the outer core and inner core have in common?

d What is the temperature of the inner core?

e What causes the Earth's magnetic field?

  Complete the table containing information about the different types of rock.

Rock type	Brief description on how they are formed	Example rocks
		Basalt, granite
	Formed from matter that has been laid down on the Earth's surface and compressed over time.	
Metamorphic		Marble, slate

  Marble, chalk and basalt are all used in buildings. Which one is an example of:

a a sedimentary rock **b** an igneous rock

c a metamorphic rock?

5 Match the label to the part of the rock cycle.

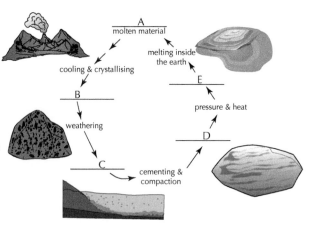

1 Magma inside the Earth's crust.

2 The rock changes to form metamorphic rock.

3 Erosion produces sediments which get washed away.

4 Igneous rock.

5 Sedimentary rock is formed.

6 Add the labels to the diagram of a volcano.

lava   magma chamber   ash cloud   crater

7 Which of the following statements is false?

A 90% of the world's volcanoes are located in the Pacific Ocean.

B There are over 1500 active volcanoes in the world.

C Volcanoes erupt every 10 years.

D Volcanoes erupt when the Earth's core moves.

8 Which of the following is not released during an eruption?

A gas

B fossils

C lava

D ash

9 Which of the following describes a dormant volcano?

A A volcano which will never erupt.

B A volcano which erupts every year.

C A volcano that has not erupted for a long time, but might again.

D A volcano that has recently erupted.

10 Which of the following causes earthquakes?

    A A shift in the plates of the Earth.

    B The moving magma in the Earth's mantle.

    C A volcanic eruption.

    D A large thunderstorm.

Exercise 17B Weather and climate

This exercise includes coverage of:

N3 Solar System

CL3 Processes of the planet SCN 3-05b

1 Describe the difference between weather and climate.

2 Which of the following are measured as part of weather predictions?

    humidity   precipitation   cloud cover   temperature   wind speed   air pressure

3 What is meant by these terms?

a greenhouse gases

b climate change

c global warming

4 Write a list of **four** factors that contribute to global warming.

5 The table shows changes in CO_2 concentrations in the atmosphere and in global average temperatures between 1900 and 2010.

Year	CO_2 concentration (ppm)	Temperature °C
1900	296	13·5
1910	299	13·5
1920	304	13·8
1930	307	13·7
1940	311	14·2
1950	313	14·0
1960	317	14·4
1970	325	14·6
1980	339	14·7
1990	354	14·9
2000	369	14·9
2010	389	15·0

Use the information in the table to draw a graph to show how:

a CO_2 levels have changed between 1900 and 2010

b temperatures have changed between 1900 and 2010.

Exercise 17C Sun and Moon

This exercise includes coverage of:

N3 Solar System

1. How many hours does it take for the Earth to spin once on its axis?

2. In which direction does the Sun set (east or west)?

3. Which way round does the Earth spin?

4. Is the daytime shorter or longer in summer than in winter?

5. How long does it take for the Earth to make one complete journey round the Sun?

6. How many times does the Earth spin on its axis while it rotates once around the Sun?

7. What force keeps the Earth in orbit around the Sun?

8. At what angle is the Earth tilted on its axis?

9. Draw a diagram to show the positions of the Earth and the Sun when it is summer in the northern hemisphere.

   > **Hint** Your diagram should show the position of the Earth's axis of rotation.

10. Why do people living close to the North Pole experience nearly 24 hours of daytime in the summer?

11. Name the **eight** different phases of the Moon.

12. How long does it take for the Moon to orbit the Earth?

13. Copy and complete the diagram to show the different phases of the Moon.

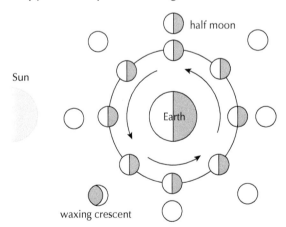

14 The photograph shows the surface of the Moon as seen from the Earth over an hour. What motion is responsible for the changing appearance of the Moon?

- **A** The Sun moving into the shadow of the Moon.
- **B** The Moon moving into the shadow of the Earth.
- **C** The Sun moving into the shadow of the Earth.
- **D** The Sun moving into the shadow of the Moon.

15 What is represented by this diagram?

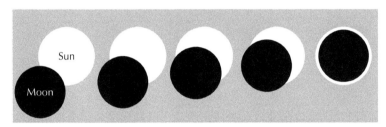

- **A** The phases of the Sun.
- **B** The phases of the Moon.
- **C** A lunar eclipse.
- **D** A solar eclipse.

16 Which of the diagrams shows the positions of the Earth, the Sun and the Moon during a solar eclipse?

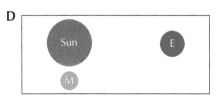

(The Earth is labelled E. The Moon is labelled M.)

17 **a** The table shows the tidal ranges at a seaside location in the course of a month. Draw a bar chart to illustrate this data.

Moon phase	Date	Tidal range (m)
◯	1	10·7
◑	3	11·5
	5	10·8
◑	7	9·2
	9	7·5
◑	11	6·6
	13	8·8
●	15	11·1
	17	12·8
◑	19	11·3
	21	9·1
◐	23	5·9
	25	7·6
◑	27	9·9
	29	10·8

b Draw the phases of the Moon above your chart.

18 Describe the difference between the position of the Earth and the Moon during a spring tide compared to a neap tide.

Hint	A diagram might help you answer this question.

Exercise 17D The Solar System

This exercise includes coverage of:

N3 Solar System

1 Name the eight planets in our Solar System.

2 What is the difference between a meteor and a meteorite?

3 What is a comet?

4 Use the information in the table to answer the questions.

Planet	Diameter (km)	Distance from the Sun (million km)	Time to orbit the Sun (days)
Mercury	5000	58	88
Venus	12 000	108	225
Earth	12 800	150	365
Mars	6800	228	687
Jupiter	143 000	780	4330
Saturn	121 000	1400	10 800
Uranus	51 000	2900	30 600
Neptune	50 000	4500	59 800

a Which planet has the largest diameter?

b Which planet has the longest year?

c Which planet is nearest the Sun?

d Which planets are larger than the Earth?

e There is an asteroid belt between Mars and Jupiter. Estimate the distance from the Sun to the asteroid belt.

f What is the relationship between the distance from the Sun and the time taken for one planetary orbit?

g Which planet do you think is the coldest? You must explain your answer.

5 A pupil writes the following information on flash cards to help revise for a test. Each statement has errors. Rewrite the statements correctly.

A The Sun orbits the nine planets of the Solar System.

B The order of the planets from the Sun is Mercury, Venus, Mars, Earth, Jupiter, Saturn, Neptune and Uranus.

C There is a rocky asteroid belt between the inner planets and the outer planets – between Jupiter and Saturn.

D The planets closest to the Sun have the longest orbit time.

E The planets closest to the Sun are on average colder than the outer planets.

F Our Solar System is part of a galaxy called the Milky Cluster.

18 Cosmology

Exercise 18A Cosmology

This exercise includes coverage of:

N4 Cosmology

N4 **1** Match the astronomical object to its description.

Astronomical object	Description
Planet	All of matter, space and time.
Moon	A planet that orbits a star outside our Solar System.
Star	A huge sphere of gas that emits light and heat.
Solar System	A huge collection of stars, dust and gas, held together by the force of gravity.
Exoplanet	A star and all the objects that orbit around it.
Galaxy	A natural satellite that orbits a planet.
Universe	A large object that orbits a star.

N4 **2** List these astronomical objects in order of size, starting with the smallest.

galaxy   **planet**   **universe**   **star**

N4 **3**   **a** Use the information in the table to plot a suitable graph to show the different diameters of the planets in our Solar System.

   b Use the information in the table to plot a suitable graph to show how the period of orbit around the Sun varies with the distance from the Sun.

Planet	Mercury	Venus	Earth	Mars	Jupiter	Saturn	Uranus	Neptune
Diameter (km)	5000	12000	12800	6800	143000	121000	51000	50000
Distance from Sun (million km)	58	108	150	228	780	1400	2900	4500
Period of orbit (days)	88	225	365	687	4330	10800	30600	59800

N4 **4** Explain what is meant by the term **light year**.

N4 **5** State the speed of light.

N4 **6** Calculate the distance, in metres, that light will travel in 1 year.

> Hint   1 year is 365 days = 31536000 seconds.

N4 **7** Calculate the distance, in metres, that light will travel in 6 years.

N4 **8** The star Vega is 27 light years from Earth. Calculate the distance in metres from Earth to the star Vega.

9 The star Proxima Centauri is 4·2 light years from Earth. Calculate the distance, in metres, from Earth to the star Proxima Centauri.

 10 The Milky Way is 100 000 light years across. Calculate the diameter, in metres, of the Milky Way.

 11 The star Andromeda is 2.1×10^{22} m from Earth. Calculate how long it would take to reach Andromeda from Earth, travelling at the speed of light.

Exercise 18B Space observation and exploration

This exercise includes coverage of:

N4 Cosmology

CL4 Processes of the planet SCN 4-06b

  1 Read the information then answer the following questions.

When you look at the stars in the night sky, they often appear to twinkle. This happens because the Earth's atmosphere bends the light coming from the star, making them flicker. Scientists cannot study twinkling stars and so telescopes have been developed that orbit the Earth, removing the clouds and the air from the observations.

The Hubble Space Telescope, which is controlled from Earth, has given astronomers very clear images of space. The Hubble Deep Field is an image of what was thought to be an empty section of sky. It has revealed stars and galaxies and is used to study the early universe.

The James Webb Space Telescope is a large infrared telescope that will study every phase in the history of our universe, ranging from the first luminous glows after the Big Bang, to the formation of solar systems capable of supporting life on planets like Earth, to the evolution of our own Solar System.

a Why do some stars appear to twinkle?

b How have astronomers solved the problem of twinkly stars?

c Name the two different telescopes.

d Using your knowledge of physics, describe what is meant by the term **Big Bang.**

This exercise includes coverage of:

N4 Cosmology

CL4 Processes of the planet SCN 4-06b

N4 **1** Which of the descriptions in this list best describes an exoplanet?

    A The object must orbit a star.

    B The object must have a moon.

    C The object must have a breathable atmosphere.

    D The object must emit light.

    E The object must be in the Milky Way.

    F The object must be part of a group of objects.

    G The object must have liquid water on the surface.

N4 **2** Explain what is meant by the term **Goldilocks zone**.

N4 **3** Use the information in the diagram to explain a method for detecting exoplanets.

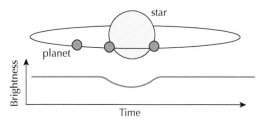

4 The aim of the Mars Rover 2020 mission is to find life on Mars. The rover will drill down about 1-2 metres and analyse the rocks under the surface. Any life would be protected from harmful radiation and may have access to underground water supplies.

This mission has a price tag of about US$2·1 billion.

State **one** advantage and **one** disadvantage of exploring Mars.

5 Use an online search engine to find out how many exoplanets have been discovered.

6 Trappist-1 is a group of at least 7 exoplanets orbiting a star which is 39 light years away from the Solar System. All the planets were discovered using the transit method. The planets were discovered from the regular and repeated shadows they cast.

The orbital periods and the sizes of the planets have been calculated. The planets have similar sizes and masses. They receive about the same about of light as Venus because of the distance at which they orbit the star.

Use your knowledge of physics to comment on the above.